JIM PALMER: NINE INNINGS TO SUCCESS

A HALL OF FAMER'S APPROACH TO ACHIEVING EXCELLENCE

JIM PALMER: NINE INNINGS TO SUCCESS

A HALL OF FAMER'S APPROACH TO ACHIEVING EXCELLENCE

* * *

Jim Palmer

with

Alan Maimon

TRIUMPH
BOOKS

Library of Congress Cataloging-in-Publication Data
  Names: Palmer, Jim | Maimon, Alan.
  Title: Jim Palmer : nine innings to success : a Hall of Famer's approach
    to achieving excellence / Jim Palmer with Alan Maimon.
  Description: Chicago, Illinois : Triumph Books LLC, [2016]
  Identifiers: LCCN 2015051125 | ISBN 9781629372266
  Subjects: LCSH: Palmer, Jim | Baseball players—United
    States—Biography. | Pitchers (Baseball)—United States—Biography.
  Classification: LCC GV865.P34 A3 2016 | DDC 796.357092—dc23 LC
    record available at http://lccn.loc.gov/2015051125

This book is available in quantity at special discounts for your group or organization. For further information, contact:
  Triumph Books LLC
  814 North Franklin Street
  Chicago, Illinois 60610
  (312) 337-0747
  www.triumphbooks.com

Printed in U.S.A.

ISBN: 978-1-62937-226-6

Design by Sue Knopf

Photos courtesy of Baltimore Orioles unless otherwise indicated

In loving memory of my parents,

Moe and Polly Wiesen,

and my stepfather, Max Palmer

Contents

FOREWORD

I'VE KNOWN JIM PALMER SINCE I WAS A 15-YEAR-OLD spring training batboy for the Baltimore Orioles, a role I played from 1970 to 1972. One of the reasons I went into broadcasting was because I saw in that clubhouse how the greatest players, on perhaps the greatest franchise in the era, went about their business... and I wanted to be a part of it by interviewing them.

The Orioles were about perfection. They had an astute and resourceful front office. They had a brilliant and mercurial manager in Earl Weaver and they had one of the most intelligent teams I've ever been around—before or since. The Robinsons—Brooks and Frank—Mark Belanger, Dave Johnson, heady players like Paul Blair, Andy Etchebarren, Boog Powell, and one of the most cerebral pitching staffs ever, featuring Dave McNally, Mike Cuellar, and, of course, Jim Palmer.

Perfection isn't possible. We're all flawed and mortal, and sports only magnifies our mortality and foibles. But the *pursuit* of perfection is what the Orioles were about. That's why I think Jim Palmer, then and now, best personifies "The Oriole Way." As a Hall of Fame player, broadcaster, and corporate spokesman, Jim has always been meticulous and passionate about excellence. He has an obsessive attention to detail and an almost superhuman compulsion to do things the right way.

"Cakes," as we called him, and many still do, had matinee idol looks, an incredible work ethic, preternatural athletic gifts, and a deliberate, methodical approach to everything he did and does. Those qualities didn't just manifest themselves on the pitching mound. He found excellence in public speaking, broadcasting, and baseball. He was the face of Jockey underwear for an astonishing 19 years, a spokesman for The Money Store for 12 years, and he's currently in the midst of a 16-year relationship with Nutramax Laboratories. There's a reason he has had such long relationships with these entities. He wasn't merely a celebrity endorsing a product. Jim Palmer understood his brand and what being a brand ambassador meant. He represented the companies and himself with integrity, consistency, and smarts.

Jim Palmer was one of the most graceful and elegant players I've ever known. He had an impeccable pitching motion and delivery. He's insightful at the microphone and articulate and thoughtful in everything he's approached. Some people looked at Jim as an almost flawless, majestic type of person. Those who viewed him this way don't know his real story. They don't know about his personal evolution.

Jim was adopted. As you'll read in this book, he grew up in a loving family, but he never knew his true roots. He broke into the major leagues at age 19 and almost immediately was celebrated as the young star who outdueled the great Sandy Koufax in the 1966 World Series. But then things went south for him. He suffered devastating arm and shoulder injuries, which almost ended his career as dramatically as it had started. I remember Jim Palmer in the minor leagues when he was struggling to pitch. I vividly remember people in the media writing him off as washed up. He was just 21 years old.

Jim went through a pair of divorces, and, though he was and remains a doting father to Jamie and Kelly and grandfather to Maxine and Henri, the failure of those marriages haunted him. He was no longer "Perfect Palmer." In fact, he would be the first to tell you...he never was.

That brings me to one of the most inspiring parts of the Jim Palmer story. Jim was married for a third time, to Susan Earle, a divorced mother of an autistic son named Spencer. Many men of Jim Palmer's pedigree would not marry again, particularly a man well into his 60s to a woman with a child who required special attention.

Not Jim.

I've seen Jim around his stepson, and, believe me, he is there every day with enormous support, love, patience, and commitment. Jim and Susan nicknamed Spencer "Indy" after Indiana Jones, one of

Spencer's favorite movies and obsessions. At Jim's statue unveiling at Oriole Park at Camden Yards, Indy introduced his stepdad in a hilarious and touching way. When Jim got to the microphone, he was so moved that he could hardly get through his speech. I've seen Jim talk many times about Spencer. Almost every time he does, his eyes fill up and his voice grows thick with emotion.

In 2013 Jim Palmer put some of his awards up for auction. The proceeds went to charity and the people who most needed the money. *That's* the Jim Palmer I admire most. He's been labeled as perfect and aloof, even distant. That's not the Jim Palmer I've ever known—and I've known him since I was a teenager.

In this book Jim Palmer candidly discusses his greatest achievements, the roads to success, the hardships and personal struggles, and why—even now—the pursuit of perfection is the underlining ingredient in the "Nine Innings to Success." Pursuing perfection isn't just elusive. It's unattainable. But in that pursuit can come excellence.

Jim Palmer's story and *Nine Innings to Success* is about that. It's about a personal commitment to be the best, about setting a plan and following it, and doing things the right way. It won't always end with a plaque in Cooperstown, but the prize isn't really at the end of the road. The prize is in the road to getting there.

—Roy Firestone
Sports commentator and
former host of ESPN's *Up Close*

INTRODUCTION

I REMEMBER MY FIRST MINOR LEAGUE START LIKE IT WAS yesterday. It came in 1964 in Aberdeen, South Dakota. I walked the leadoff hitter and, after the opposing team pulled off a successful hit-and-run, I had to deal with runners on first and third with nobody out. At that point I couldn't help but think, *Boy, am I in over my head!* Facing my first real test as a professional ballplayer, I got the next three hitters to strike out, pop out, and fly out. Disaster averted, I settled down and went on to win the game.

Nobody remembers how I pitched out of a jam in my first inning at Single A, but I certainly do. Throughout my career I would look back on that day as a reminder that success is a process based on thousands of moments, events, and outcomes. A couple of years later, when I got the ball in Game 2 of the 1966 World Series at Dodger Stadium, I faced a challenge not unlike the one the first time I pitched in Aberdeen—different scale, of course, but same mind-set. Though I was still a few days shy of my 21st birthday, I felt prepared to go up against the legendary Sandy Koufax on the biggest baseball stage imaginable.

In a few short pages, I'll start walking you through what I call the "Nine Innings to Success." As you'll soon find out, "walking" is a key word here. Before I became the youngest pitcher to ever throw a shutout in the World Series, won 20 games in a season, or secured a spot in the Baseball Hall of Fame, I was a skinny kid averaging more than a walk an inning in the minor leagues. And even after I experienced my first taste of big-time success in the major leagues, I nearly saw my career end prematurely due to injury.

Along the way, you'll hear a lot about Earl Weaver and the other colorful characters I crossed paths with during my career as a player, broadcaster, and corporate spokesman for Jockey underwear, The

Money Store, and Nutramax Laboratories. Earl and I had plenty of dustups, but our mutual admiration for each other and our commitment to common goals led to amazing success in the workplace. Despite our differences I like to think that I made Earl a better manager in the same way that he made me a better player. If only Howard Cosell had been present to do the play-by-play of some of our confrontations, now that would have been entertaining. My work with Howard, Al Michaels, and Tim McCarver in the ABC broadcast booth taught me a lot about relationships and workplace dynamics. It also gave me an ample supply of great stories.

I want to celebrate the game. I want to celebrate life. Each has its challenges, detours, joys, and moments of sadness. By adhering to a set of essential values, I believe we can take control of our own destinies and prepare ourselves for successful relationships and careers. I'm not naïve. I've seen too many people suffer too much adversity to think that anything is a given. I know there are no guarantees in life. Sometimes misfortune is unavoidable. But life's unpredictability is why it's imperative to take the steps necessary to control what we have control over.

I was fortunate to play on teams that ranged from very good to outstanding. In my 19 years in Baltimore, the Orioles posted a losing record only once—in 1967, a season when our pitching staff was decimated by injury. But in my current capacity as a television broadcaster for the team, I've seen the Orioles struggle through some lean times. I still feel greatly invested in the team's fortunes and think a lot about the concepts of winning and losing and success and failure.

You're not always going to win. In baseball that's easily quantifiable. The team with the best single-season record in baseball history, the 1906 Chicago Cubs, lost 36 times during the regular season and fell in the World Series. On an individual level, the best hitters ever to wear a uniform made far more outs in their careers than they got hits.

Edward Bennett Williams, who owned the Orioles from 1980 until his death in 1988, helped me develop my ideas on what it means to be successful. He viewed the subject from the vantage point of an attorney who had fought many difficult and unpopular battles during a distinguished legal career. Winning and losing are not as black and white as they always appear, he said. In baseball the scoreboard tells you which team is ahead. But sometimes the final score doesn't tell you the whole truth—just as a jury verdict doesn't always tell you how well you argued your case. He made me realize that "How did you lose?" is a question that should be asked more often. Were you prepared? Did you commit yourself physically, emotionally, and intellectually to maximizing your potential? Did you do your best? If you answer those questions affirmatively, you should be able to live with whatever the outcome is. Williams liked to say you should put yourself in a position to live your life with "no I's and no R's" or no indecision and no regrets.

Even in a Hall of Fame career, you get into ruts. You'll read about times in my life when success seemed effortless and other times when just lifting my arm was a struggle. As a starting pitcher, I was handed the ball every four days and asked to go out and do a job. I had my fair share of 1-2-3 innings, but I also had to work my way out of a lot of jams. Going the distance was my objective every time I took the mound. I liked the challenge of trying to get a hitter out the fourth time he came to the plate to face me. And if you totally commit yourself to a goal both mentally and physically, you have a much better chance of achieving it. That was a pillar of "The Oriole Way," which helps frame many of the discussions in this book.

The Orioles fielded some of the best teams in baseball during my playing career. Between the 1968 and 1985 seasons, we never finished with a losing record, a stretch that included six American League pennants and three World Series. That streak of winning seasons is the second longest in baseball history. You can't win as many games as we did without talent. But our organizational culture played an equally significant role in our success. For the moment I'll single out two players who exemplified "The Oriole Way": Brooks Robinson and Cal Ripken Jr. Like me, they played their entire careers in the Orioles organization. You don't see that much anymore in sports—or any other industry in America. I'm not here to promote blind loyalty, but I do believe that a positive organizational culture helps energize people and make them more successful. I'm proud that I wore the same No. 22 Orioles uniform for my entire career.

This book will address other questions, including: What do I want to achieve? What do I need to know to achieve it? How do I establish myself in the workplace? How do I react when I face an obstacle? How do my relationships with others help me succeed? What steps do I take to achieve true excellence? After I learn to perform at a high level, what do I need to do to sustain that level of achievement? Is it ever too late to try and establish myself in another field? And what role do gratitude and humor play in all of the above?

Not everybody experiences "nine innings" in the same order. I had already experienced success in the major leagues by the time I faced my greatest period of adversity in the form of injuries that sidelined me for the better part of two seasons. The steps I took to resume my career taught me perseverance. Cal and Oprah Winfrey's hard times—yes, they both had them—came at the beginning of their careers, but both overcame early obstacles to achieve true greatness. More on that later.

Dr. Bill Engelhart, a friend of mine who was an obstetrician, and I used to playfully argue about the degrees of difficulty of our respective professions. He argued that his job was infinitely harder than mine. And I playfully disagreed. "Does the wind ever blow out in the operating room when you're delivering a baby?" I would ask jokingly. Of course, baseball is just a game, and its results are frivolous when compared to the work product of many other professions. But sports offer a unique window into how we as a nation do business. Baseball is predicated largely on the physical skills of unusually talented individuals, but it's the mental component of the game that keeps us so enthralled. Did the general manager construct a good team? Does the manager handle his team well and make smart strategic decisions? Is the team focused, prepared, and ready to fulfill its potential? Those are questions that apply to any workplace.

I played the game and have lived my life by a set of core principles and I look forward to sharing the wisdom and strategies that helped me excel on and off the baseball field.

Well, it looks like the managers are out on the field swapping lineup cards. It's a beautiful day for baseball. There's a cloudless sky, and it's 75 degrees. Or maybe it's not. In the game and in our lives, sometimes we bask in the bright sunshine, and other times we get poured on. If you're lucky, you'll have a guy like my former Orioles teammate Rick Dempsey around on those stormy days. Nobody made a summer downpour more entertaining than Rick. At the end of the day, a sense of humor is what sustains us. But you'll have to wait until the ninth inning to hear more about that.

So let's play ball.

1ST INNING

Learning

L IFE IS ABOUT OPPORTUNITY. AND IF SUCCESS IS important to you, you'll have no qualms about going wherever that opportunity surfaces. With that in mind, let's take a trip back in time to the summer of 1963. The location: a tiny hamlet in southern South Dakota called Winner, a rural outpost tucked away off a lonely stretch of highway somewhere between the towns of Mission and Ideal. One name seemed to be a misnomer; the other had some symbolism. Was the location ideal? No, not really. But was I on a mission to become a winner? Yes, absolutely.

Of all the summers of my youth, this one shaped up to be the most pivotal. I had just graduated from Scottsdale High School in Arizona, where I starred in baseball, football, and basketball. On the diamond I had established myself as enough of a prospect to earn a chance to try out for the Basin League, which was halfway through a two-decade run as a showcase for the nation's top amateur talent. I ended up making the team. Of all the players who passed through South Dakota that summer, I was the only one who hadn't entered college yet. My teammates in Winner included future Cy Young award winner Jim Lonborg, who at the time was just a humble biology major at Stanford.

The Winner Ritz-Carlton must have been booked because my teammates and I were all piled into the basement of a house with no air conditioning. The outside temperature would get up to 90 or 100 degrees during the day, creating a sauna-like atmosphere in the basement. Late at night, however, it cooled off enough to allow us to sleep through until mid-morning. At around 10:00 AM, there'd be a knock at the basement door, and the poor guy, who I'm guessing juggled owner, general manager, manager, and wake-up call duties, would tell us to get up and report to our jobs, which the NCAA required that we have. *Job?* I didn't know I had one. But when I arrived at the ballpark and was handed a rake, I figured it out pretty quickly.

My routine in Winner was simple. Before games I raked the mound. And during games I stood on the mound and hoped opposing hitters didn't rake my pitches. That's how the summer went. We ended up losing in the Basin League playoffs, but my performance got the attention of Orioles scout Jim Russo and Harry Dalton, who ran the organization's farm system. It also drew the interest of Paul Richards, who had recently resigned as Orioles manager to become general manager of the Houston Colt .45s. I met with representatives from both teams when I returned home to Scottsdale, Arizona, and ended up signing a $40,000 contract with the Orioles. That was the best decision I ever made. As I once said in *Sports Illustrated*, if I had played my career for the Houston Astros, who didn't win their first pennant until I was 60 years old, I would likely have had a good but not great major league career.

> The stock market, like baseball, has its ups and downs. Both games are nuanced, mandate concentration, and require mentors to elevate individuals to their highest potential. There's tough love involved in the mentoring process. A mentor in the financial world will call you out for not being rigorous enough in your research—just as a good baseball man will make sure you practice your pitching or hitting.
>
> My Grandma Koufax (Yes, that Koufax!) was painfully honest in her mentorship of me. When sharing her investment knowledge, her favorite phrase was, "Don't piss in my eye and tell me it's raining."
>
> There is no substitute for hard work, but we all need mentors like Grandma Koufax or Earl Weaver to keep us on the straight and narrow, so that we can constantly improve our investing prowess, our skills on a baseball field, or our efforts in any area in which we strive for excellence.
>
> **—DOUGLAS A. KASS, PRESIDENT, SEABREEZE PARTNERS MANAGEMENT INC.**

I'll get back to South Dakota shortly. But for the moment, let's move down the map to Thomasville, Georgia, the town where the Orioles used to send their low-level minor leaguers for an eight-week intensive course in the fundamentals of the game. In Thomasville, I got my first introduction to "The Oriole Way." And from the day in 1964 that I showed up to camp there to the day that I retired from the game in 1984, I remained immersed in those principles. They shaped my career—and, to a significant extent, who I am. It wasn't an accident that I never played a game for another professional organization.

In Thomasville the players didn't live in a basement. In what may or may not have been an upgrade from cellar dwelling, they assigned us to an old army barracks that shared property with a facility that housed a bunch of World War II veterans. We dined in a mess hall and were roused from bed each morning by a bugle call. In that militaristic environment, the likes of Earl Weaver, who managed the Orioles' Double A farm club in Elmira, New York, and Cal Ripken Sr., who helmed a minor league team in Aberdeen, South Dakota, served as our MacArthur and Patton. They imparted a number of lessons, including that Orioles farmhands didn't cut corners. During an intra-squad scrimmage, I lined out to right field to end an inning. I ran hard out of the batter's box but only made it halfway to first base before the outfielder snared the ball. At that point, I turned and headed to the dugout, where I grabbed my glove and went out to the pitcher's mound. That night at dinner, one of our instructors, I think it was Earl, called me out in front of all the players for my perceived lack of hustle. "Did you run that ball out?" he asked me. "We run balls out in the Oriole organization. We run all the way to first."

This was the first time I laid eyes on the little pudgy guy whom I would come to regard as both a nemesis and a genius. Earl had run the Thomasville camp since 1961. I didn't get to know him well that spring and I don't recall seeing his explosive temper on display either. I just remember we had an incredible two months. I learned a lot about the game from Earl, Cal, and the other instructors. And their teachings paid immediate dividends. Pitted against other teams' best young players, we won 14 games in a row.

I thought I would have the chance to spend more quality time with Earl in 1964, but instead of getting assigned to his Double A team in Elmira, I received instructions to report to Cal's A ball squad in northern South Dakota. The town of Aberdeen had mosquitoes the size of B-52 bombers, but it also had a great mentor who taught me life lessons that I would constantly harken back to as I went through my career. Cal distilled his message into a few commandments.

You're never going to let anyone outwork you.
You're going to be a great teammate.
You're going to have fun—and part of having fun is winning.
You're going to have a passion to get a little better every day.

Cal also reminded us to always credit the people who made it possible for us to play the game professionally in the first place: the fans. Without them we were just guys playing baseball in an empty stadium. It's worth mentioning that Cal's four-year-old son, Cal Jr., joined us for the summer and soaked it all in. As I watched him run around the field before games, I thought to myself, *Someday, this kid is going to play in 2,632 consecutive major league games.* I'm kidding, of course. But there is definitely something to be said for growing up an Oriole.

At 18, I was one of the youngest players on an Aberdeen roster that featured nine future major leaguers. I roomed with Dave Leonhard, who was 23 and a college graduate. Davey and I didn't have a whole lot in common on paper, but we hit it off really well. Davey not only possessed a bachelor's degree in history, but he also had obtained it from one of the nation's premier institutions of higher learning, Johns Hopkins University. The baseball season at Johns Hopkins consisted of about 12 games, which was the precise number of times scouts didn't show up to watch Davey's team play. Upon graduation he put his degree to use by teaching high school English in the Baltimore area. It never crossed his mind that he would have a shot at playing professional baseball. But a chance encounter with an Orioles scout named George Henderson at a local sporting goods store changed the direction of his life. Henderson had watched Davey pitch in a church league against a team he was monitoring and thought enough of what he saw to offer him a contract. This was in the spring of 1963. Davey politely declined the offer, citing his contractual obligations to the school that employed him. When the scout informed him that he wouldn't have to report to his rookie league team in Bluefield, West Virginia, until June, Davey changed his mind. "I needed to find a summer job anyway," he told me soon after we met. Whereas I signed for $50,000, Davey received no cash bonus, but the scout did help him get a 20 percent discount on the spikes he was looking at in the sporting goods store that day. He also encouraged Davey to change his date of birth on the contract so that he wouldn't get heat for signing a player of such advanced years.

Part of the reason why Davey and I became such quick friends is because our teammates viewed us both with a degree of suspicion. Some guys resented that I had signed for a significant amount of money, and they looked for signs that I was pampered and unwilling to pay my dues. I made sure they couldn't find any. Davey was a bit more erudite than everyone else on the team. That opened him up to the scorn of his lesser educated brethren. But he, too, proved that he was willing to outwork anybody. Neither of us drank or partied much with our teammates, getting the most out of our $3 per day in meal money. That, too, fed our outsider status. Davey and I remain great friends to this day.

Cal Sr. treated all of his players the same, but he was enough of a talent evaluator to know which of us had the potential to go places. He also recognized that talent and potential alone weren't enough to take a player from A ball to the majors. An aspiring major leaguer needed discipline and focus, too. I remember one night after an extra-inning game in St. Cloud, Minnesota, when some teammates and I went to a pool hall down the street from our hotel. Our 12:00 AM curfew was approaching, but we thought we could squeeze in a couple of games. Right around the stroke of midnight,

I was at the table about to strike the ball when my cue bumped up against a wall. Except it wasn't a wall. It was Cal, who looked none too pleased that I wasn't back at the hotel. "There are suspects, and there are prospects," he said. "Prospects make curfew."

"Yessir," I replied before putting the cue back on the rack and walking out the door.

The Aberdeen club started out something like 25–4 and cruised to a league title while cruising around the Upper Midwest (and Canada) on a rickety old school bus. I tied for fourth-most wins on the team with 11 and threw a no-hitter, but I also walked 130 batters in 129 innings and led the Northern League in wild pitches. Davey, the "college boy," led our staff with 16 wins. When I threw strikes, I kept opposing hitters at bay. But I didn't throw nearly enough of them. As crazy as it sounds, I had no idea where the ball would go when it left my hand. Obviously, that is a huge stumbling block for a pitcher who hoped to make the majors. I needed help and, over the next couple of years, I would get it from some of the best baseball minds around.

Billy Hitchcock, the former Orioles manager who served the organization as a roving instructor, took me aside after one of my starts in Aberdeen. If it was like most of my outings, I probably struck out four, walked nine, and got the win. He introduced himself and told me he liked my velocity. Then he asked me a question: "Has anybody ever told you that you don't have to throw every pitch as hard as you can?" As a matter of fact, nobody ever had. I took his comment to heart.

The old adage about baseball being a game of failure is true. Take a starting pitcher who loses four out of every 10 games over the course of a lengthy career or a veteran everyday player who fails to get a hit seven out of every 10 times he comes to the plate. There's a pretty decent chance that at least one of those players is going to end up in Cooperstown. Even the best major league pitchers aren't going to get wins every time out, and the most talented major league hitters are going to be retired far more often than they reach base.

If you can't accept and move on from failure and disappointment, you'll drive yourself crazy with frustration.

In 1964 I played with Lou Piniella in Aberdeen and in the Florida Instructional League. You couldn't miss Lou in the dugout because he would lose his mind every time he made an out. I mean he'd really go crazy, smashing his batting helmet against the dugout wall until it split in two. After lining out with the bases loaded to end an inning, Lou stormed back to the dugout and took his anger out on the helmet. As the spectacle unfolded, our second baseman Bobby Litchfield said, "You know, Lou, just relax. Even if you hit .300, you're going to break seven out of 10 helmets. With the kind of money we're making, I'm not sure you can afford that." Lou started laughing. He controlled his temper enough to enjoy a successful major league career in which he hit around .300 every season. All his bottled up emotions didn't boil to the surface until Lou became a manager and threw some Weaver-like tantrums on the field.

In June of 1964, the Orioles and a select group of the organization's high-level minor leaguers came to Aberdeen to play an exhibition game against us. Sometimes you get humbled, and this was one of those times.

My teammate Eddie Watt, who dominated the Northern League that season with a 14–1 record, got the start. I remember that Eddie's dad had hopped in his car and driven up from Sioux City, Iowa, to watch his son go up against major leaguers. Facing the likes of Brooks Robinson and Boog Powell, Eddie didn't fare well at all. I forget how many runs they scored off him, but I distinctly remember a downtrodden Mr. Watt getting up from his seat in disappointment after an inning and a third and driving back to Sioux City.

I didn't throw a pitch that day, but I still got a real education, watching established major league pitchers like Milt Pappas and Steve Barber having an easy time with our lineup. We all get afflicted with self-doubt from time to time, and I found myself overcome by a wave of uncertainty that day. I was coaching first base late in the game when our opponents brought in a Double A pitcher named Steve Cosgrove. He had a zippy fastball that seemed to accelerate an extra couple of miles per hour as it neared the plate. And he had a curveball that absolutely dropped off the table, freezing batters and buckling their knees. It was one thing watching the mastery of All-Stars like Pappas, who had won at least 10 games in a season every year since he was a rookie, or Barber, who won 20 games in 1963, but Cosgrove was a 20-year-old minor leaguer playing for Earl Weaver in Elmira. I silently mused, *If they throw like that at Double A, how are you supposed to ever get to Triple A or the big leagues?*

As I observed him from the first-base coaching box in Aberdeen, I didn't know the whole story about Cosgrove. It turned out that he was a lot like me as a young pitcher. He could blow away hitters with his fastball, but he struggled with control. Some pitchers can work through that kind of problem, but Cosgrove's high-strung personality didn't mesh well with Earl's managerial style. When he pitched for Earl at Elmira, and later at Triple A Rochester, he would let Earl get into his head. Whenever he threw a couple of balls to a hitter, Earl would grumble, "Here we go again!" In Earl's complicated mind, those represented words of motivation. He signified his trust in you by sending you out to the mound. What you did out there was up to you. Cosgrove had the tools to be an accomplished pitcher, but at the end of the day, he could never pitch effectively for Earl. He never made it out of the minor leagues.

There's a simple lesson there: you can have all the natural ability in the world, but you have to figure out a way to channel your talent—and to forge at least serviceable working relationships with those in charge. I'll return time and again in the pages of this book to Earl Weaver and his leadership style. I figured out early on in my major league career how to deal with Earl's bluster, but I recognized that not everybody had that same capability. Life and baseball can be unforgiving, and we all know a few Steve Cosgroves, people who had extraordinary ability but, for one reason or another, couldn't get over the top.

Did Earl Weaver destroy the confidence of his players with his sharp tongue and crusty personality? Yes, that had to be considered an occupational hazard of playing under Earl. But it doesn't do him justice. He was a great player development guy during his time in the Orioles' minor league system and, when he became skipper of the Orioles after the All-Star break in 1968, he invested himself fully in trying to get the most out of his players. But here's the most important thing you need to know about Earl: he didn't want you to like him...And he didn't want to like you. In his mind any type of kinship between player and manager prevented him from being a true leader. I'm not sure I fully agree with that opinion, but it certainly worked for Earl.

Earl knew when to suppress his baser instincts in order to help build a player's confidence. A great example of that came in 1977 when my friend and former teammate Mike Flanagan was struggling in his first full season in the big leagues. Through his first 13 starts, Flanny had a 3–8 record, and his mind was racing. Mike was a bit of an introvert, the type of person who you might not realize is extremely witty and bright if you didn't take the time to get to know him. There was one thing he wanted more than anything else in the world: Earl Weaver's approval. He told me as much as we sat next to each other on a United Airlines charter flight from Cleveland to Boston in the summer of '77. We were back in coach, by the way. Earl, as was customary, occupied a seat in the first row of first class, even though he didn't need the extra legroom. "Earl doesn't have faith in me," Flanagan lamented, puffing on a cigarette.

"I don't think that's the case, Flanny," I replied. "You're not pitching real poorly, and he keeps sending you out there."

"Yeah, but I'm used to Joe Altobelli," Flanny said, referring to his soft-spoken manager at Triple A.

"You're not going to get that kind of love from Earl," I told him. "He's not that type of guy. Keep doing what you're doing, and things will improve."

The next day, when we arrived at Fenway Park, I paid a visit to Earl's office. I told Earl about my conversation with Flanny. It didn't sit well with Earl. "*Confidence?*" he repeated. "That cocksucker's killing us. He's 3–8, but I keep sending him out there, don't I?"

"Are you going to keep doing that?" I asked.

"Well, yeah, I don't have anybody else."

"So call him in and tell him you have faith in him."

Somewhat to my surprise, Earl heeded my advice and even took it a step further. He didn't just tell Flanny he believed in him. He told the world.

"I don't care what Flanagan's record is," Earl said the next day in an interview with a sportswriter from *The Boston Globe*, who was checking up on Flanagan, a New England native. "He's going to be a winning pitcher in the big leagues."

Earl didn't lie to make people feel better. He truly believed that Flanagan could be a successful major league pitcher. For all the negativity he spewed, Earl also recognized when a player needed a nudge. After *The Globe* story ran, Flanny reeled off five straight complete-game victories and finished the season with 15 wins and 10 losses.

But back to my formative years in the minors. After a season of Single A ball in Aberdeen, I reported to the Florida Instructional League. As a high school kid back in Scottsdale, I used to gawk at the bonus babies who showed up in Arizona to play in the Instructional League there. They would hang out at the Safari Hotel on Scottsdale Road, which had the best coffee shop in town. You could spot the young ballplayers from a mile away. They drove nice cars with out-of-state plates and all wore Sansabelt slacks and Alpaca sweaters and Ban-lon shirts. In 1964 I was one of them, albeit in a different sunny location.

I didn't go to Florida to work on my tan. I hoped to keep improving my game and I couldn't have asked for a better setting to accomplish that goal. Then-Orioles manager Hank Bauer and his top coaches all came to Florida to tutor us. We'd go on the field at 8:15 in the morning and stay out there until the sun went down, working on every facet of the game. One morning as I was putting on my sanitary socks, I thought to myself, *There must be something I can do today to make them notice me.* I'm not sure the guys on either side of me had that same thought. In fact, a lot of guys were bitching and griping about being out on the field until it was dark out. I wasn't taking names, but I'd venture to guess that a fair number of the complainers never made it in the big leagues. To me, it was a question of attitude. While others viewed the all-day sessions as a chore, I saw them as an opportunity to prove myself in front of the most important talent evaluators in the organization. By impressing those individuals, I could earn a ticket out of A ball and all that came with it: the long bus rides, the $3 a day in meal money, and the living in a basement. The same applies to every job. It doesn't matter what you do or who you work for. You go to work every day and you have a chance to make your supervisor think, *You know what, I've got a real special employee.*

I once asked Mike Ditka for his thoughts on what makes people successful. He said, "Jim, it's simple. Anybody can make a commitment, but the people who set themselves apart are able to *keep* the commitment." And I think he's absolutely right. Can you dot the i's and cross the t's? How hard do you want to work? How much do you care? The answers to these questions help determine who thrives and who doesn't.

I think they noticed me in the Instructional League but maybe not for all the right reasons. Like in Aberdeen, I won more games than I lost and had a sub-3.00 ERA, but I walked 60 batters in 53 innings. Thank goodness for George Bamberger, whose impact on my career started in Thomasville, Georgia, and continued through the glory years in Baltimore, when he oversaw a pitching staff with four 20-game winners in 1971. George, who was a minor league pitching instructor in 1964, evaluated my strengths and weaknesses as a pitcher and worked with me to change my windup. He would send me down to the bullpen without a baseball to work on keeping my balance as I went into my delivery. I would do that exercise over and over again. With my mechanics in better working order, I had a much easier time finding the strike zone. From there George instructed me on the finer points of locating my pitches, especially the art of throwing down and away to right-handed hitters. Through repetition of these exercises, I made myself a markedly better pitcher. And I also learned a valuable lesson that I would harken back to often in my career: practice doesn't make perfect; perfect practice makes perfect.

Remember how I once marveled at the quality of pitchers at Double A? Well, my next stop after the Instructional League wasn't Double A Elmira. And it wasn't Triple A Rochester either. At the age of 19, I became a member of the Baltimore Orioles. My newfound ability to throw strikes helped put me on the fast track to the big leagues, but injuries to some key pitchers on the Orioles staff also led to my promotion. I made $600 a month that season up from $500 a month in 1964. It took me seven tries to get the raise. Each time Orioles general manager Lee MacPhail sent me the $500-a-month contract, I'd send it back, hoping he would reconsider and give me a slight pay bump. Finally, on a friend's suggestion, I told MacPhail that my wife was pregnant, which she wasn't. That broke the stalemate, and I got the extra cash. About a year later my wife did get pregnant, so my conscience is clean. I didn't get a dime more for going 17–4 in A ball and Instructional League but earned an extra $100 for lying about my wife being pregnant. Go figure.

Looking back on my quick ascension to the big leagues, I think about guys like Cosgrove and Steve Caria, a pitcher whom I first met playing Babe Ruth League ball in Hawaii as a kid. We had a lot in common. We were both born in October 1945. We both threw right-handed. We were roughly the same height and weight. And we both ended up in the Orioles organization as teenagers. Caria got assigned to the Orioles' Class A team in Fox Cities, Wisconsin, where he had 195 strikeouts in 154 innings, including 20 in a single game. Like me, he earned an invitation to play in the Winter Instructional League. There, he continued to perform at a very high level. We both made the big league club's 45-man roster, and he easily could have gone to the majors over me. I think I got the nod because I could handle myself with the bat and had better all-around athletic ability. Caria ended up a career minor leaguer.

My roommate for the first half of the 1965 season was 38-year-old Robin Roberts, who found himself at the tail end of a 286-win career. It was no accident that the team paired him up with a rookie half his age. The Orioles knew that Robin could help further my education as a young ballplayer. And I didn't pass up the chance to pick his brain at every opportunity. Late nights on the road, I'd ask him about the craft of pitching. He would roll over in bed and say, "Kid, I'm 38 years old. I need to get some sleep. I'll answer that question in the morning." Because he wanted to get some rest, Robin's message was to the point: "The fastball is the best pitch in baseball. You've got a great one. And I hope you're smart enough to use it." Echoing Bamberger, Robin told me that I needed to think less about the velocity of my pitches and more about their location. He assured me that the ability to throw a well-placed fastball would translate into a lot of major league wins.

Robin and I met different fates in 1965. I pitched mostly in relief during my rookie year, proving to myself and the organization that I deserved to stay in the majors. Though he didn't pitch that poorly, going 5–7 with a 3.38 ERA, the Orioles released Robin at the end of July. I was sorry to see him go. The few months I spent with him had a profound impact on me.

During his peak years with the Philadelphia Phillies in the 1950s, Robin would come in and pitch in relief on days when he wasn't starting. Those appearances enabled him to pick up a few saves to accompany 20-plus wins. Robin lived to compete. He made 609 major league starts and completed 305 of them. From a baseball standpoint, Milt Pappas, another of my teammates in '65, was the antithesis of Robin Roberts. And watching Milt go about his business in my rookie season imparted a lesson as valuable as any other I learned that year.

In addition to being a nice guy, Milt possessed one of the best sliders in baseball history. When I saw him pitch the previous summer at the exhibition game in Aberdeen, I marveled at the movement on his pitches. But here's the thing I learned about Milt after reaching the big leagues: if he started a game and held a lead after five innings, he wouldn't hesitate to ask the manager to remove him from the game. In baseball parlance that's called "five and fly."

By pitching five innings, Milt had qualified for a win and he saw no problem with leaving his fate in the hands of his bullpen.

A game he started in September 1965 at Yankee Stadium stands out in my mind. Facing Whitey Ford in the first game of double-header, we held a 2–1 lead after the fifth inning. The only New York Yankees run came on a solo homer by leftfielder Tom Tresh. With Tresh on his way to the plate to lead off the bottom of the sixth, Milt called our catcher, Dick Brown, out to the mound. "There's something wrong with my stomach," Pappas told Brown.

Brown beckoned our manager, Hank Bauer, to join the conversation.

"It must have been something I ate," Milt explained to Hank. "I need to come out."

Bauer honored Milt's wish and removed him from the game. Dick Hall relieved him and pitched four perfect innings to preserve a 2–1 win. When the team piled into the clubhouse after the game, Milt was sitting there, munching on a piece of pizza and slurping a Yoo-hoo, looking like the happiest guy in the world. Our manager felt a less positive emotion upon seeing Milt binging on junk food. "Get the hell out of here!" Bauer barked at him. "Go sit in the bullpen! I don't even want to look at you!"

I was 19, and Milt was 26 still in what should have been the prime of his career. What he did at Yankee Stadium was a revelation to me. I felt I needed to probe his mind-set. A few days after that game, I asked him about his goals and ambitions. To my surprise he told me he was contemplating retirement. "But Mr. Pappas," I said deferentially, "you've never played in a World Series or won 20 games in a season. Isn't there more you want to accomplish?"

No, he told me. He felt totally content winning 15 or 16 games a season. And he didn't feel the fire in his gut to keep playing. "You can still make a lot of money even if you don't win 20 games," he said.

The $15,000 bonus a pitcher could get back then for winning 20 games in a season wasn't a bad motivator, but that notwithstanding, Milt's attitudes felt totally foreign to me. In my way of thinking, the people who put their trust in me to win games deserved better.

And the fans who paid their hard-earned dollars to watch me pitch deserved better, too. But equally important, I wanted to live up to the standards of the outstanding players who came before me—the Koufaxes, the Wynns, the Fellers, the Fords, the Drysdales.

It might sound like I'm getting on Milt, but I really did have tremendous respect for him as a pitcher. Though he never ended up winning 20 games or pitching in a World Series, he finished with more than 200 victories in his career and pitched a no-hitter for the Chicago Cubs. He was nothing if not consistent, notching double-digit wins almost every season he pitched. And he did throw 129 complete games in his 17-year career. (I went the distance 211 times in 19 seasons.) He was even honored with a Milt Pappas Day by the Cubs, for whom he played the last four years of his career. But judging Milt on his own words, finishing what he started wasn't his goal each time he went out to the mound.

From Robin and Milt, I soaked up a lot of knowledge in 1965. Some of it helped shape me into the ballplayer I wanted to be, and some of it, well, let's just say I never, ever wanted to be a five-and-fly guy.

As a reliever and spot starter in 1965, I spent a lot of time in the bullpen, chatting with the veterans who sat beside me. That season the Orioles had a backup catcher named Charlie Lau, who went on to become one of the great hitting instructors the game has ever seen. In 1969, Charlie's only season as hitting coach for the Orioles, he worked with shortstop Mark Belanger on a regular basis. Whatever Charlie told him to do must have worked. Mark's batting average skyrocketed, and he struck out half as many times as the season before. When Charlie left the Orioles the next season, Mark's average plummeted again. For a single season, Charlie turned a career .228 hitter into a .287 hitter.

Charlie nicknamed me "Brash" because I was so inquisitive. But how could I have passed up the opportunity to ask questions? I had an entire volume of human encyclopedias sitting around me. I can't overemphasize the importance of seeking out the advice and wisdom of others when you're young and green. My early years in the Orioles organization taught me how to be mentored, and in turn it made it a given that I would later be a mentor to future Orioles pitchers like Flanagan, Scotty McGregor, Mike Boddicker, Storm Davis, and Dennis Martinez. And that didn't make me special. What I did for the pitchers, Eddie Murray, Ken Singleton, Al Bumbry, and Lee May did for young position players. "The Oriole Way" was an everyday reality, not just an abstract philosophy. And it worked.

While it's possible to get ahead in life all on your own, it sure helps to have mentors and teachers showing you the way.

VISIT TO THE MOUND

"It's not what you know. It's who you know." I think we've all heard that saying before. That's a little too cynical for my liking. So let me offer a twist on the old aphorism that I think more accurately applies to anyone embarking on a career or just interested in becoming better at what they do: "It's not what you know or who you know. It's who you know and taking the time to find out what they know."

We'd like to think that we have all the answers, but none of us do. Even the most accomplished people still have things to learn about their chosen fields. Michelangelo, the Italian Renaissance artist whose masterworks adorn the Sistine Chapel in Rome, is a great example. Late in his career, he purportedly uttered the Italian phrase, "Ancora imparo." The English translation is: "I am still learning."

Michelangelo had it right. So did Earl Weaver when he famously said, "It is what you learn after you know it all that counts." And that philosophy is as relevant today as ever. Eric Schmidt, executive chairman of Google and a true 21st century visionary, put his own spin on the sentiment when he told Time magazine, "We run the company by questions, not answers." Asking questions is a sign of strength, not weakness. Great leaders know that and so should anybody who strives for greatness."

What is your "WHY"? Before you jump to how to reach a goal, first get clear on your WHY. Your WHY is what will pull you toward your goal. Model the behavior of those who have already done what you want to do. Brainstorm different ways to reach your goal. There doesn't have to be a master plan—just a menu of strategies for achieving your objectives. Be creative. Compare brainstorming to the menu at a restaurant. You're only going to order one or two things, but there's a whole array of choice in front of you.

Whether you've been in the workplace a year, 10 years, or 30 years, there are always new concepts, strategies, and skills to learn. We normally think of the mentor-mentee relationship consisting of an older worker mentoring a younger one. But in this computer-reliant day and age, the script often gets flipped, creating an even more valuable opportunity for older and younger workers to learn from each other.

Seek out those who know more than you do and ask them questions. Don't be shy. While not all accomplished people like to share their experiences and give advice, I find that most do. Try it out. Approach a more seasoned colleague at an opportune time and ask him/her a work-related question that's been on your mind for a while. That conversation could lead to many more. And make sure you return the favor. One day you will be in a position to mentor less experienced colleagues. Remember the wisdom and expertise that others shared with you and the role it played in getting you where you are.

2ND INNING

Becoming Successful

M Y ROOKIE SEASON EASED ME INTO LIFE IN THE BIG leagues. I pitched in 27 games, starting six times, for a 94-win Orioles team that finished third in the 10-team American League. Today that win total would almost guarantee a team a spot in the postseason. In the winner-take-all days of 1965, however, we came up nine games short of winning the pennant and advancing directly to the World Series. It was a thrill to see myself on a baseball card for the first time. The only problem was my card incorrectly listed me as a southpaw.

My first win came on May 16, 1965, when I pitched three and two-thirds innings of one-run ball in relief against the New York Yankees at Memorial Stadium. This was before the designated-hitter rule went into effect, and I took advantage of my chance to swing the bat by swatting a two-run home run off of Jim Bouton, who, in addition to being a pretty decent pitcher, would go on to write the famous baseball book *Ball Four*. Speaking of balls and strikes, my most notable accomplishment in 1965 was finding command of the strike zone. I walked 56 batters in 92 innings, a vast improvement over my wild days in the minors when I averaged more than a walk per inning. There were moments in my rookie season when I felt like I belonged in the big leagues—like the time I struck out the great Al Kaline in my first career start—and other moments when I thought I couldn't compete at the highest level—like the time later in that same game when Kaline hit a home run off of me. Everything was still new to me, including my own team. On our first road trip of the season, I picked up a copy of the *Boston Herald* and read little bios in the sports page of all the Boston players. As I quickly got up to speed on the backgrounds and accomplishments of the Red Sox, I realized that I knew more about them than I did about our own guys.

I had no idea where my baseball career would take me, so every time I went to the mound, I tried to savor the moment. Remember the scene in the movie *City Slickers* where Billy Crystal's character, Mitch Robbins, and his two pals drive a herd of cattle across the plains and swap stories about their greatest days ever? Mitch reminisces about the time his father took him to Yankee Stadium for the first time and how he marveled at the greenness of the grass, which looked much more drab on his family's black and white television. Mitch talks about how it was the first game he saw in color, an experience that was punctuated by watching Mickey Mantle hit a home run. I could relate. In June 1954 my dad took me to my first game at Yankee Stadium. Allie Reynolds pitched a complete-game shutout, Mickey got three hits, and the Yankees trounced the Cleveland Indians 11–0. That was my first "Billy Crystal moment." I went home that night sure in my mind that I wanted to become a ballplayer.

Fast forward 11 years to Labor Day 1965, when I experienced my second such moment. I'm standing on the mound of Yankee Stadium for the first time, making a long-relief appearance. There are two on and two outs in the bottom of the second inning when my childhood hero Mickey Mantle steps up to the plate. And I strike him out. It was then that I realized that my childhood dream had come true.

As a team we stood on the verge of true excellence. Dating back to its days as the St. Louis Browns, the Orioles franchise had never won a World Series. All the right pieces, though, seemed to be falling into place by 1965. Brooks Robinson, Boog Powell, and reigning Rookie of the Year Curt Blefary powered our offense, and our young pitching staff showed it could hold its own against American League lineups. But something, or more accurately, *someone* was missing. In the competitive American League, we needed another top-flight player to put us over the top. As the Orioles devised a way to acquire that missing piece, I got an up-close glimpse at a young slugger who would go on to become baseball's biggest attraction of the 1970s.

My relationship with this future star started on a summer day in 1965 when I drove past Druid Hill Park in Baltimore and saw a young man wearing an Arizona State Sun Devils baseball jersey. Having attended high school in Scottsdale, Arizona, I had seen such jerseys many times but never before in Baltimore. I stopped my car, rolled down the window, and asked the kid where he got the jersey. He told me that he attended ASU and played baseball and football there. He had come to Baltimore to play on an amateur summer team managed by longtime Orioles scout Walter Youse. I asked him if he needed a lift anywhere. He told me he was going to the ballpark, so we drove over to Memorial Stadium together. That's how I met Reggie Jackson.

I later asked our new scouting director Walter Shannon about Reggie. His eyes lit up at the mere mention of the name. "If you go back to Arizona this winter, go check him out for yourself," Shannon advised. "We pick 16th in the draft next year, so we don't have a chance at getting him, but I think you'll enjoy seeing what he can do."

On a visit to Arizona that offseason, I went to watch an intra-squad scrimmage at Arizona State. Gary Gentry, a right-handed pitcher who I would go up against in Game 3 of the 1969 World Series, was pitching for one of the sides. Reggie faced Gentry four times that day. In his first at-bat, he tripled to left-center field. In his second time up, he singled and stole a base. In his third crack at Gentry, he hit a home run over the scoreboard in right field. And in his final at-bat, he singled and stole another base, giving him a 4-for-4 afternoon with two stolen bases. He also showed off his arm from center field, throwing out a runner who was trying to go from first to third on a single.

I next saw Shannon at spring training. "Did you get a chance to see Reggie Jackson while you were out there?" he asked.

"Yeah, I did," I replied, "and now I know why we don't have a chance of drafting him."

I would later have an opportunity to play with Reggie, albeit only for one season. In the 1970s Reggie became a baseball superstar, helping to turn every team he played on into a winner. The 1960s had a player of similar ability and impact. His name was Frank Robinson. And the Orioles concluded that he was the missing piece to our puzzle.

After the '65 season, our general manager, Lee MacPhail, left the organization to work in the office of the commissioner of baseball. Before heading to New York, he initiated discussions with the Cincinnati Reds about a trade for Frank, who had averaged 37 home runs a year during his 10 years in Cincinnati and who had won the National League MVP award in 1961. For reasons not entirely clear, especially considering that Frank had an outstanding 1965 season, the Reds seemed to think he was past his prime, "an old 30," as they called it. Harry Dalton, who succeeded MacPhail as Orioles GM, continued talks with the Reds and consummated the deal. The always consistent—if not overly ambitious—Milt Pappas went to Cincinnati, along with relief pitcher Jack Baldschun and outfielder Dick Simpson. In return we got a player who immediately took his game to an even higher level, winning the Triple Crown in 1966. Depending on your allegiance, you consider that deal either one of the best or worst trades in major league history. There's even a line about it in the movie *Bull Durham* uttered by Durham Bulls superfan Annie Savoy: "Bad trades are a part of baseball—now who can forget Frank Robinson for Milt Pappas, for God's sake?"

Frank's presence in the middle of our lineup promised to make us even better offensively. Defensively, we were already the class of the American League. You would need an entire room to fit all the Gold Glove awards won by third baseman Brooks Robinson, shortstop Luis Aparicio, second baseman Davey Johnson, and center fielder Paul Blair. As a fly-ball pitcher, I especially appreciated Paul's speed and range in the outfield. I wish I knew how many runs he saved me during the 10-plus years that we played together. A pitcher like me who didn't strike out a whole lot of hitters is reliant on the defense behind him. I was criticized at times for directing fielders on precisely where to position themselves, but that's not because I doubted their ability. Paul, Mark Belanger, and the other outstanding fielders who backed me up in 1966 and beyond are a big reason I'm in the Hall of Fame.

In 1966 Cooperstown couldn't have been further from my mind. I had yet to even solidify my status as a major leaguer. My second season with the Orioles presented me with a tremendous opportunity to prove that I belonged. Manager Hank Bauer clearly believed in my abilities. He wouldn't have named me to fill Pappas' spot in the rotation if he didn't. So I joined a young, entirely homegrown pitching staff that also included Dave McNally, Wally Bunker, Steve Barber, and John Miller. At 28 years of age, Barber was the old man of the staff.

Before the '66 season, the baseball writers picked the Minnesota Twins to edge us out for their second straight American League pennant. It's not a stretch to think that I might have been one of the reasons that the Orioles failed to get the most first-place votes. We compared well to Minnesota in every area except for starting

It seems nowadays that everyone is looking for a quick path to success instead of putting in the time and work necessary to climb the ladder. I challenge our Orioles coaches and players every day all the time never to be perceived as working on your next potential job. Do the one assigned to you as well as it can be done and you may be surprised where it takes you.

I managed several teams in the New York Yankees minor league system before becoming a coach and then manager of the big league club in 1992. Over the course of my managerial career, I've learned a lot through observation. Especially at the start, my exposure to others in the game showed me how to do things...and how not to do things.

As a manager and talent evaluator, I've seen a lot of young players with dreams of becoming successful major leaguers. After assessing a player's skills, I take a step back and try to answer a few questions: Do I think the player will make his teammates better? Is there a "competitive sincerity" about him? Will he be a part of positive peer pressure in the clubhouse or will he be a sympathetic ear to less positive elements in the locker room?

Not many of us become overnight successes. It's a step-by-step process. And it's important to remember that someone is always observing us.

—**BUCK SHOWALTER, ORIOLES MANAGER AND THREE-TIME AMERICAN LEAGUE MANAGER OF THE YEAR**

pitching, where the Twins had established veterans Mudcat Grant and Jim Kaat pitching every four days. The presence of an unproven 20-year-old hurler in the Oriole rotation couldn't have escaped the attention of the press corps. Thankfully, championships are won on the field, not awarded by writers. In our pursuit of the pennant, at least we didn't have to worry much about the Yankees, who, after advancing to the World Series every year from 1960 to 1964, had entered a period of mediocrity that would last until the late 1970s.

I got the ball in the second game of the '66 season against the Red Sox and in front of fewer than 2,000 fans at Fenway Park I took a shutout into the bottom of the ninth inning. I ended up going the distance in an 8–1 win. I hit the second of my three career home runs in that game. I also threw 177 pitches. We started the season with two wins in Boston, dropped a game at home to the Yankees, and then reeled off 10 straight victories. In early June we passed the Indians and moved into first place for good. On September 22, 1966, I notched a complete-game victory against the Kansas City A's that clinched the Orioles' first ever postseason berth. The game ended on a fabulous diving catch by center fielder Russ Snyder—yet another reminder of the role great defense plays in winning games. There wasn't really much of a pennant race that season. We finished the season nine games in front of the second-place Twins.

I paced our young staff with 15 wins. I didn't quite achieve ace-level status. No one in the rotation did. But our starters kept us in games, and our bullpen, which led the American League in saves, usually held onto leads. And our offense took care of the rest. Frank Robinson's Triple Crown season included 49 home runs, 122 RBIs, and a .316 batting average. The numbers don't tell the whole story of Frank's dominance that season. During a game in May, he became the only player to ever hit a ball out of old Memorial Stadium. Not just over the outfield wall. *Completely out of the stadium.* The ball ended up under a car in the stadium parking lot. Frank became the unanimous choice for American League MVP, making him the only player to date to win the award in both leagues.

How potent was our lineup in '66? Boog Powell and Brooks Robinson, who hit immediately behind Frank in the lineup, finished second and third in the MVP balloting. On any given day, one or more of those three would put on a show. But as with all winning teams, we also got timely contributions from role players, who hit key home runs or delivered wins in spot starts.

Our World Series opponent, the defending champion Los Angeles Dodgers, clinched the National League pennant on the last day of the season, and most people felt they would repeat as champs, a feat that no team besides the Yankees had accomplished since 1930. The Dodgers had two huge reasons to like their chances: Sandy Koufax and Don Drysdale, the standard bearers for pitching in the early and mid-1960s. Between 1962 and 1966, they combined for 209 victories in the regular season. Do the math on that one. That's an average of almost 21 wins apiece. And their brilliance carried over into the postseason, where they had led the Dodgers to championships in 1963 and 1965.

Because I split my childhood between New York City and Southern California, the Dodgers were the closest thing I had to a hometown team. I'll talk more about my upbringing later in the book, but a thumbnail version of it will help you understand my connection to the Dodgers. When I was nine years old, my adoptive father, Moe Wiesen, died suddenly of a heart attack. We were living in Rye, New York, at the time. Soon after he passed away, my adoptive mother, Polly Wiesen, in search of a fresh start, picked up and moved me and my older sister with her to Southern California. Not long after we all landed in the Los Angeles area, so, too, did the Dodgers. I know the move from Brooklyn to L.A. broke a lot of hearts back east, but for me, the team's westward migration gave me a taste of the home I left behind after my father's death.

As a teenager in California, I remained true to my first love, the Yankees, but I also developed a strong affinity for the Dodgers. I regularly went to games at the Los Angeles Coliseum, the stadium that the team called home until Dodger Stadium opened in 1962. I would sit out in the left-field stands and watch home-run balls soar over the so-called "Chinese wall," which was just 251 feet from home plate. By contrast the right-field foul pole was 440 feet from home. How cavernous was right field? I remember sitting in the

Coliseum and watching Junior Gilliam of the Dodgers score all the way from second base on a Carl Furillo fly ball that the Philadelphia Phillies' Richie Ashburn chased down. Wally Moon of the Dodgers adjusted his entire approach to hitting based on the Coliseum. As a left-handed hitter, Moon recognized what he was up against in that place, so he learned to launch balls to the opposite field, quickly gaining fame for hitting towering "Moon shots" over the Chinese wall.

I remember watching the opening game of the '63 World Series between the Dodgers and Yankees on television. I couldn't wait to see what kind of offensive attack the Yankees could mount against Koufax. As it turned out, it wasn't very much of one. Koufax went into Yankee Stadium like he owned the place and struck out 15 to put the Dodgers up in the series. The Yankees never recovered from that humbling experience. Sandy came back with another overpowering performance in Game 4 to finish off the sweep, giving the Dodgers their second World Series since leaving Brooklyn. I observed enough of Sandy in that series to know that he was the kind of pitcher I aspired to be.

I had long admired the Dodgers as a fan. Now, a couple of weeks shy of my 21st birthday, I was scheduled to pitch against them in the second game of the World Series.

On paper the '66 Fall Classic looked like a battle between our bats and the Dodgers' arms. Speaking in favor of the latter, the sportswriters noted that our entire pitching staff had completed 23 games in the regular season, while Koufax alone had gone the distance 27 times. The Dodgers also had a clear edge in experience. Almost everyone on their team had played in the World Series, whereas we had just three players with postseason experience: Aparicio, Frank Robinson, and reliever Stu Miller.

I honestly didn't think we had much of a chance of winning Game 1, regardless of who the Dodgers chose to send to the mound. That's no knock on Game 1 starter Dave McNally; it's just that they were the Dodgers. Manager Walter Alston opted for Drysdale because Koufax had clinched the pennant for the Dodgers on two days' rest on the final day of the season, and a start in the opening game of the series would have required pitching him again on short rest. That meant I would face Koufax in Game 2.

McNally was a quiet and tenacious guy who went on to enjoy an excellent major league career that included four consecutive 20-game seasons. But in 1966, like me, he was still just a kid. Drysdale might have been coming off of a subpar season by his standards, a 13–16 record with a 3.42 ERA, but he was still one of the preeminent pitchers in the game.

In Game 1 McNally struggled to pitch off of the high Dodger Stadium mound. Normally a pitcher with outstanding control, he walked five hitters in the first two and one-third innings. Bauer had him on a short leash. In fact, I was the only pitcher on the team not sitting in the bullpen, making me unavailable to come in at the first sign of trouble. After McNally walked the bases loaded in the bottom of the third, Bauer gave him the hook. Fortunately, we had grabbed an early lead off Drysdale, thanks to back-to-back home runs in the first inning by Frank and Brooks. So when Moe Drabowsky took over for McNally, we had a 4–1 lead.

Nobody could have foreseen what happened next. Before I talk about the unexpected performance that took place that night, I should give it some context by saying a few words about Drabowsky. When Moe first broke into the majors in 1956, he showed real promise as a starting pitcher, but arm problems early in his career seriously reduced his effectiveness. By 1966 he had drifted into journeyman status. At 31 years of age, he had knocked around the majors for a decade, suiting up for the Chicago Cubs, Atlanta Braves, Reds, and Oakland Athletics, never once coming close to reaching the postseason. Better known for his comedic personality and the pranks he pulled on teammates than for his accomplishments on the mound, Moe would make long-distance calls from the bull-pen phone—quite possibly to his native Poland—if that was even possible. He liked to put snakes in teammates' lockers and earned the title "King of the Hotfoot" for good reason. On the night we clinched the American League pennant, we drained every bottle of champagne in the visitors' clubhouse in Kansas City, so Moe called a local liquor store, did his best impersonation of Orioles owner Jerry Hoffberger, and ordered another six cases.

Moe might have been a jokester, but he was no fool. To supplement his baseball income, he worked as a stockbroker during the offseason. After the St. Louis Cardinals put him on the scrap heap in the fall of 1965, before he ever suited up in a game for them, Moe considered retiring. But the opportunity to play for a pennant contender in Baltimore persuaded him to stick it out at least another year. We acquired him off waivers for $25,000. In his first season with the Orioles, Bauer relegated him to the bullpen, where he performed well, mostly in the long-man role.

Would a guy who had considered calling it quits before the '66 season to become a full-time stockbroker crumble under the pressure of pitching in his first postseason game or would he meet the challenge of a crucial long-relief stint in the World Series?

From the get-go, Moe showed he was up to the challenge. He contained the damage in the third inning, allowing only one run to cross the plate. We still led 4–2. After that he settled into a once-in-a-career type of groove, striking out the side in the fourth and fifth innings. The rest of the guys sitting in our bullpen didn't have to get up for the rest of the day. Moe finished the game, striking out 11 (all swinging) while allowing only one hit, a single. We took Game 1 by a score of 5–2. A *Chicago Tribune* columnist corralled Moe after the game and was rewarded with a quote that was pure Drabowksy: "Just what is a guy like me doing in fast company like this?"

Success is contagious. When people around you show grit and grace under pressure, it inspires you to do the same. Moe's dominating outing in Game 1 of the World Series influenced me in a way I couldn't have articulated at the time. Looking back, however, the lesson I learned from his performance is crystal clear: regardless of where you've been or where you're going, when you encounter a challenge that calls for your best, you either embrace the moment and perform up to or even beyond your ability or you spend the rest of your life regretting what might have been. Moe turned in one of the most clutch pitching performances in Orioles history, and I saw no reason why I couldn't follow suit. Though I had spent only a brief time in the majors, I had learned my craft from some of the best teachers in the game. They believed in me, and I felt I owed it to them to reward that faith. At the very least, I didn't want to embarrass myself.

The mound I pitched from at Scottsdale High School was 60' 6" from home plate and so were the mounds I pitched from in the minor leagues and in my first seasons in the majors. The dimensions of the infield and the rules of the game don't change in October, but the magnitude of the games sure do. More often than not during the '66 season, I pitched in front of sparse crowds of 15,000 or fewer. In Game 2 of the World Series, I would be going out in front of a capacity crowd of more than 55,000 at Dodger Stadium.

Prior to the game, I could visualize myself on that mound. I had learned as much as I could about the habits of the Dodgers hitters, a process that included studying how Moe had tamed them the night before with mostly fastballs and reading the advance report of our super scout Jim Russo, whose research made me feel like I had pitched in the National League all season.

There's a thin line between being tense and intense, uptight, and ready. I knew that I was backed by a talented team, but I faced the great unknown of how good I would have to be to keep pace with Koufax. At best, according to my calculations, I had little margin for error. At worst, I had none. Sandy and I both faced the impediment of nagging discomfort in our pitching arms. I had felt stiffness in my right shoulder for most of the second half of the season, but I didn't think much of it. I figured that I had aggravated a tendon while painting the interior of my house in August. I was only making $7,500 a season and couldn't afford to pay somebody else to do the job. To ease the pain, our team doctor gave me a shot of cortisone a day or two before my World Series start. Sandy had long suffered from arthritis in his left elbow, so the match-up featured two guys with sore arms.

I didn't have any trouble sleeping the night before the game. Despite the enormity of the situation, I felt an inner calmness. The whole thing had a surreal quality to it. I wanted to enjoy the experi-ence—not feel stressed out by it. On gameday Sandy and I posed for a United Press International photo together. He seemed like a really nice guy. There's another photo of me from that day, cutting into a stack of 40 or so pancakes, my pregame meal of choice, which earned me the nickname "Cakes." I'm not sure I finished the entire mountain of pancakes, but it did make for a great photo op.

After all the hoopla, I felt relieved when the game actually started. My first pitch didn't go to the backstop, which was also a huge relief. And with each passing pitch, I felt more comfortable out there. By the fifth inning, neither team had put a run on the board. Other than having to work out of a bases-loaded jam in the second inning, I felt very much in control. And by the looks of it, so did Koufax, who was accomplishing the difficult task of making our hitters look human.

I made it a point earlier in this chapter to single out the Orioles' defense for praise. For all the pre-World Series talk of the Dodgers' pitching and our offense, Game 2 of the '66 Fall Classic turned on defense—poor defense by our opponents. In the top of the fifth inning, Dodgers center fielder Willie Davis got caught in a waking nightmare. He lost two fly balls in the sun and, after muffing the second, airmailed a throw to third base, giving him a World Series-record three errors in the inning. Those errors led to three unearned runs. Davis' teammates chipped in with another three errors on the day, making for a total of six. I don't care who the pitcher is. He's going to have a tough time overcoming that kind of sloppy play. It is amazing how one bad inning of baseball can define a player in people's eyes. The first line of Davis' obituary in the *Los Angeles Times* referred to him as "a brilliant but sometimes erratic center fielder." He won three Gold Gloves for the Dodgers, but he never quite lived down that fateful day in October 1966.

Already up by three runs, we tacked on another run in the sixth on a Frank Robinson triple and a Boog Powell single. From that point on, it was just a matter of keeping my composure and seeing through what I started. And that's what I did. I got John Roseboro to pop out to shortstop for the 27th and final out of the game, putting the finishing touches on a 6–0 win and my best performance to date in the majors. Until that day I hadn't thrown a shutout in the big leagues. I soon learned that I had just become the youngest pitcher ever to accomplish that feat in the World Series. My stepfather, Max, was in attendance for the game. Long after the other fans had filed out of the stadium, he remained in his seat. He later explained that he never wanted to let go of the moment. I consider that win against the Dodgers the most memorable of my career. The combination of the occasion, the performance, and the opponent make it hard to top. It boosted my confidence, taught me the importance of not being intimidated, and, most importantly, helped convince me that I wanted to be an Oriole for life.

A year earlier the Dodgers had dropped the first two games of the World Series in Minnesota before coming back to beat the Twins in seven. But we took the opening games on the road and believed we wouldn't have to make a return trip to Dodger Stadium if we kept playing the way we had out west. The goal was in sight: win two out of three in Baltimore, and we would be World Series champs. Our two wins in L.A. had clearly impressed our hometown fans. Thousands of people flocked to the airport in the middle of the night to welcome us back.

In the next two games of the series, we scored a total of only two runs and had a total of just seven hits, but incredibly, that ended up being enough to win both contests. We took Game 3 by a score of 1–0 behind Wally Bunker's pitching and a home run by Blair. McNally then went out and blanked the Dodgers 1–0 to finish off the sweep. To put that into perspective, the run that the Dodgers put on the board in the third inning of Game 1 was the last they scored for the entire series. They crossed the plate a total of two times in four games. In the end it wasn't the Dodgers arms or the Orioles bats that carried the day. It was the young Orioles pitching staff.

The front page headline of the October 10, 1966, edition of *The Baltimore Sun* said it all: "Would You Believe It? Four Straight!" A lot of my teammates still have that front page framed and hanging somewhere in their homes. Beneath the headline is one of the all-time great sports photos (okay, I'm a little biased) showing Brooks leaping with joy, suspended in midair as McNally and catcher Andy Etchebarren celebrate near the mound. *The Sun* compared the revelry on the streets of Baltimore after our victory to the celebrations in the city that followed our declaration of victory in World War II. Over the years Milt Pappas, who didn't last very long in Cincinnati after his trade there, has maintained a sense of humor about the indirect role he played in making us so successful in 1966. "It was nice of me to give them a World Series," he quipped at an Orioles event not long ago.

Players, like the fanbase that cheers them on, never forget a franchise's first world championship. For that reason 1966 holds a special place in my heart and the hearts of Baltimoreans of a certain age. As it turned out, the heights we reached in 1966 represented an important step toward making us a model franchise. On a personal level, it was especially meaningful because my contributions to our success helped me earn the respect of my veteran teammates. After the World Series, Stu Miller, one of our best relievers, told *The Sun*, "I don't want to hex Jim by rating him with Sandy Koufax, but I'll tell you this—Jim is going to be around a long while. He'll go quite a way. He has a straight overhand motion that gives him plenty of zip. He doesn't have a great move to first, although that will come in time. He thinks out there, too." I considered Stu one of the great multi-inning closers ever to play the game, so his praise meant a lot to me.

As I said before, talent goes a long way toward determining success, but it's not the only ingredient, especially in an organizational setting. The '66 Orioles shared an essential trait with the other championship teams that I later played for: each player on the team recognized he was a part of something bigger than himself. As a result we played with pride, drive, and motivation, elements that poor and dysfunctional teams sorely lack.

About a month after he pitched against me in the World Series, Koufax shocked everybody by announcing his retirement at the age of 30. Most fans knew he had traumatic arthritis in his left elbow, but the outstanding results he was still getting on the mound suggested he had the ailment under control. Apparently, that wasn't the case. In order to pitch, Sandy had to ingest a medicine cabinet worth of anti-inflammatories, get his arm shot up with cortisone, and bathe his elbow in an icy bath after games. The chronic pain in his elbow had rendered everyday activities difficult, and he worried that he would do permanent damage to his arm if he continued pitching. He acknowledged that the Dodgers' team physician had encouraged him to quit before the '66 season.

The baseball community understandably reacted with dismay to the news that it would never again see the "Left Arm of God" throw a pitch. I felt honored to have pitched against him in his final game. Based on his career achievements, he deserved a better outcome in that one. After the series Koufax gave an interview in which he pretty well summed up the life of a pitcher: "Look, I could rest and wait until my arm felt fine before I pitched. Then I'd win maybe 10 or 12 games a year, and my team would finish fourth. What kind of sense does that make? I think most pitchers have to face some kind of pain during their career. It's a question of degree. You accommodate to it."

It's true that the type of injury that shortened Koufax's Hall of Fame career can happen to anybody. I know because, as I was still basking in the glow of winning the 1966 World Series, it nearly happened to me.

VISIT TO THE MOUND

Before you can travel the road to success, you need to find an on-ramp. I knew from a young age where I wanted my metaphorical highway to take me: Yankee Stadium, Fenway Park, and all the other major league ballparks in the country. By working hard, honing my craft, and applying my natural talent, I was fortunate enough to get where I wanted to be. I realize, however, that the search for the ideal career path can be elusive for a lot of people. Ideally, we all want jobs that fulfill us emotionally, intellectually, and spiritually, and sustain us financially. That can be a high bar to get over, as many jobs check Box A but not Box B or vice versa. Once you've identified a job that checks both boxes, you can start looking for that on-ramp. When you're looking for that on-ramp, though, you're going to face roadside hazards.

In the face of difficult challenges, stay focused on the task at hand. Don't let external factors get in your head. If you've delivered a great speech in front of 40 people, there's no reason you can't deliver that same greet speech to an audience of 400 or 4,000. And when you do become successful, savor it. Remember how gratifying it feels and make a permanent mental note of the steps you took to get there.

Increase your sensory acuity. Notice what works and what doesn't. Notice the relationship between laser-like focus and the many opportunities/learning experiences that present themselves. Allow the people around you to make you better and strive to do the same for them. A rising tide lifts all boats.

There's no reason to panic if you don't know exactly what you want to do when you're in your 20s or even your 30s. An article I read in *Inc.* magazine illustrates how history is full of late bloomers. Sam Walton was 44 when he opened the first Walmart, Charles Darwin didn't write *On the Origin of Species* until he was 50 years old, and Ray Kroc was in his 50s when he launched the first McDonald's. Even the late tech entrepreneur Steve Jobs struggled to find the ideal situation to fulfill his potential. Yes, he became enormously rich and successful at Apple right out of college, but then at 30, he had to reinvent himself after being fired by the company. During a 2005 commencement speech at Stanford, he talked about how his dismissal was a blessing in disguise: "I didn't see it then, but it turned out that getting fired from Apple was the best thing that could have ever happened to me. The heaviness of being successful was replaced by the lightness of being a beginner again, less sure about everything. It freed me to enter into one of the most creative periods of my life."

I echo that sentiment. The first few miles you travel on a career path can be the most important and rewarding. The newness of the experiences, the thrills of the initial triumphs, and the "lightness of being a beginner" are all wonderful parts of the journey. I got on the on-ramp when I signed with the Orioles in 1964 and didn't exit the highway for another 20 years. I hope that each of you enjoy similar longevity in your careers. But first you need to match up your talents and passions with an appropriate opportunity. That could lead to a long career in one industry and increase your chances of having a fulfilling work life, as opposed to just a job that pays the bills.

3RD INNING

Perseverance

S O LET'S START WITH THE OBVIOUS. WINNING A WORLD Series is very cool. Baltimore's 1966 title carried extra meaning because it was the first in Orioles franchise history. The Colts and Johnny Unitas had brought the city back-to-back NFL championships in 1958 and 1959, but in an era when baseball was still very much the national pastime, the Orioles going all the way really got the city excited. Growing up watching Mickey Mantle and Yogi Berra, I had dreamed of becoming a New York Yankee. But after being a part of something so special in Baltimore, I couldn't imagine playing in any other city or for any other team. I was truly on cloud nine.

The World Series victory coincided with some major developments in my personal life, most notably an addition to my family. About a month after we beat the Los Angeles Dodgers, my wife, Susan, gave birth to our daughter Jamie. In anticipation of this momentous occasion, we had bought a three-bedroom, one-bathroom house in the Baltimore suburb of Timonium. It cost $26,200, a hefty sum for a guy making only $7,500 with the Orioles. Even with my $11,682.04 World Series share, I wouldn't have felt comfortable splurging on the $28,250 house that my teammate Dave McNally bought. Then again, he'd spent a few more years in the big leagues than me and probably had stashed away a rainy day fund.

In the process of purchasing the home, I learned a little bit about 17th century feudal law in Maryland, a lesson that ended up impacting my offseason activities. It turned out that some homeowners in the state didn't actually own the land on which their homes sat, forcing them to pay a "ground rent." I was one of those homeowners, which meant ponying up an extra $150 or so a month to the shadowy individual who did own the grounds. It was a humbling reminder that, despite my status as a World Series-winning pitcher, I was still too young to actually own my property.

Fortunately for a guy struggling to pay his ground rent and grocery bill, my World Series exploits led to some offseason opportunities to make a few extra dollars in the Baltimore area. I spoke at a lot of Little League banquets and civic gatherings, collecting a stipend of $25 per speech and 10 cents per mile traveled outside of Baltimore. I enjoyed getting out and meeting so many Orioles fans, though not everyone rolled out the red carpet for me. I remember a Little League commissioner in Hanover, Pennsylvania, got really miffed that he had to pay me an extra $8 to drive the 80 miles up to the snack food capital of America and back. He must have been a disgruntled Philadelphia Phillies or Pittsburgh Pirates fan.

Other part-time work opportunities also emerged. The Orioles organization had a close relationship with a well-known Baltimore ad executive named Herb Fried, whose clients included the National Brewing Company, owners of the Orioles. McNally and Boog Powell, among others, earned a few easy bucks singing the praises of National Bohemian, which everyone recognized as the official beer of the Orioles. After games you could always find a few cases of "Natty Boh" in our clubhouse. I would have liked to get in on that action, but I guess I looked too young and clean-cut to shill beer to the Baltimore drinking public. So I took a meeting with Fried to discuss what else he had available. "What can you do?" Fried asked me. It was freezing out, but Fried had a deep golden tan and the relaxed appearance of a man for all seasons.

"I can throw high fastballs," I glibly answered. I don't remember if Fried cracked a smile or not.

"No, I mean where can we get you a job?"

I had no idea where he could get me a job, so in order to buy some time, I complimented him on the beautiful suit he had on. Well, that settled it. He ended up placing me at Hamburgers, a local clothing store chain that was another venerable Baltimore institution. At the downtown location, I got paid $150 a week to sell clothes, work in the stock room, and sign autographs.

I met a lot of die-hard Orioles fans that winter, not all of them at Little League galas or browsing the inventory at Hamburgers. I remember going out to lunch one frigid afternoon with an older salesman who had worked at Hamburgers for decades. Stopped at a red light, the driver of the car next to ours rolled down his window and motioned for me to do the same. I obliged. "Nice game, Jim," he said in a deep, throaty rasp.

The guy reminded me of a mob boss in an Edward G. Robinson movie from the 1930s. All I could think to do was wave and say thanks. As we pulled away, I asked my clothing store colleague if he knew the gentleman in the other car. "You don't want to know," he said with a smile. I got the feeling that, whoever the guy was, my performance in Game 2 of the 1966 World Series had helped pay for *his* ground rent and most likely a few luxury items.

Other than having to endure a bitterly cold Baltimore winter, I couldn't say I had any complaints. My life seemed to be falling into place. I had a wife, a baby daughter, a home in the suburbs, and would soon be fitted for a championship ring. The best feeling of all was the excitement I felt over what tomorrow would bring personally and professionally. That's true happiness.

At spring training I got more welcome news: the Orioles doubled my salary from $7,500 to $15,000, a figure that translated into a $1,000 for each win I earned the previous season. Fifty years later a pitcher in a similar situation would be rewarded with a contract paying closer to $1 million per win. Needless to say, the game has changed a lot over the decades. But I viewed my pay bump in 1967 as a step in the right direction. Those were the days before long-term contracts when owners didn't hesitate to cut players' salaries at the slightest sign of struggle. I was going to make more money than I had the previous season. That equated to success.

When I reported to spring training, I learned that things weren't quite perfect in my life. The right-shoulder stiffness that I first felt during the '66 season continued to bother me, and even though I had rested my arm for the entire winter, the problem seemed to have worsened. I figured I would just pitch through the discomfort—possibly with the help of cortisone shots—until the pain dissipated. Time heals all wounds, I figured. Why should mine be any different?

In my first start of the '67 season, I tossed a complete-game victory versus the Minnesota Twins, bolstering my belief that I would be able to pick up where I left off in the World Series and put together another successful year. My next several starts were a mixed bag, setting the stage for a pair of outings that remain among my most memorable for very different reasons.

On May 12 at Yankee Stadium, I took a perfect game into the bottom of the seventh inning before surrendering a leadoff single to Horace Clarke. But Clarke was erased when I got the next batter, Tom Tresh, to ground into a double play. From there I retired the rest of the Yankees in order, finishing off a one-hit, near-perfect shutout in which I faced the nine-inning minimum of 27 batters. It was unlike any game I had every pitched. The pain in my shoulder prevented me from mustering any kind of velocity on my fastball, which meant I couldn't have been throwing more than 85 miles per hour. But the way I mixed up my pitches and changed speeds combined to throw the Yankees hitters completely off balance. That performance represented the personal highlight of my season—just as our 14–0 drubbing of the Yankees that day was probably the team's best showing in what developed into a disappointing and injury-riddled season, in which we finished with 76 wins and 85 losses.

Five days after taming the Yankees, I experienced every pitcher's worst nightmare during a start in Boston. With one out in the first inning, Mike Andrews of the Red Sox banged a ball off the Green Monster but was thrown out trying to make it to second. Good thing for me because the next three batters walked, singled, homered, and singled again. Pitching coach Harry Brecheen came out and asked catcher Andy Etchebarren how I was throwing. "How would I know?" Andy said, taking off his mask. "I haven't caught one yet."

I managed to get out of the inning with a strikeout. Between frames, I asked Hank Bauer to take me out. I was in severe pain. My arm felt like a useless appendage.

An orthopedist who examined me a day or two after the Boston game didn't think I had anything to worry about. He chalked up my problem to muscle fatigue possibly caused by a pinched nerve. Bauer and general manager Harry Dalton thought I might benefit from some time off, so in the weeks that followed, I underwent a regimen of heat treatment. I returned to the mound in June to test out my arm but experienced the same pain and same poor results. I lasted only three innings against the California Angels. That was long enough to know that I couldn't pass myself off as a big league pitcher in my current condition.

Things fall apart. And eight months after experiencing World Series glory, my body sure did. Bauer, a former World War II combat platoon leader, had a rub-dirt-on-it attitude toward injuries. He was convinced the problem was all in my head. I tried reasoning with him. "Okay, Hank," I said in frustration one day, "if it's all in my head, why doesn't my head hurt when I throw the ball?" He brushed off the question.

Bauer and Dalton had more than just me to worry about. They were in the midst of a season, in which four of our starting pitchers from the previous season missed significant time due to injury. The whole situation reminded me of when I was 12 years old, playing Little League in Beverly Hills, and experienced a growth plate injury that rendered me unable to pitch. Until I felt better, I had to play first base. My coach didn't like it because he wanted his best pitcher on the mound, not at first base. That scenario was now playing out at the major league level.

Unable to identify what ailed me, the Orioles assigned me to our Triple A affiliate in Rochester, New York. I didn't agree with that decision. As I said at the time, I couldn't imagine that Rochester manager Earl Weaver wanted a pitcher on his roster who was physically unable to perform his duties. It wasn't like I needed time in the minors to work on a certain pitch or gain back lost confidence. My arm hurt every time I threw the ball. I was damaged goods. And in the minors, I felt I risked aggravating the problem. My fears were realized when I found myself unable to get Triple A hitters out. In my first start at Rochester, I gave up four runs and seven hits in four and one-third innings. My next outing went even worse. I pitched two and one-third innings and yielded five runs on five hits.

Finally and mercifully, the organization put me on the disabled list—the Rochester disabled list, to be exact. That kind of peeved me for reasons dealing with major league service time and how it related to receiving a pension. At this point in my career, I couldn't take anything for granted and had to start thinking about my financial future.

The time off didn't help. After a month on the DL, the only pitching I could do was at batting practice. Thinking my shoulder might benefit from some time in the Florida sun, the Orioles assigned me to our Single A affiliate in Miami. Actually, that only partly explains why I went all the way down the minor league ladder in 1967. The other reason was that Rochester and our Double A team

> You don't know what you're made of until adversity strikes. Failure is inevitable, and fear of failure was my fuel.
>
> After 12 years in the big leagues, I faced the realization that my career as a starting pitcher was over. The Oakland A's and manager Tony LaRussa believed I had more left to offer. With Tony's confidence in me, I reinvented my career by becoming a closer and went on to pitch another 12 seasons.
>
> Two years into my comeback as a closer, I gave up a historic home run to Kirk Gibson in Game 1 of the 1988 World Series. That was failure at the highest level, on the biggest stage. Many people thought it might destroy me. But it was just one moment. I chose not to let that one moment define me, diminish from my accomplishments that season, or destroy my comeback.
>
> I stayed focused and embarked on a mission to overcome that lowlight. The very next season, we came back and won the World Series, sweeping the San Francisco Giants. I closed the deciding game and registered the final putout at first base. It was one of the greatest moments of my life.
> **—DENNIS ECKERSLEY, HALL OF FAME PITCHER**

in Elmira were competing for their respective pennants, and it was evident that I would have been a liability during the stretch run. What a difference 10 months make! I went from pitching against Sandy Koufax in the World Series to not having what it took to help a minor league team win a title. Team success at the minor league level was a tenet of "The Oriole Way." Although other organizations were happy to use their farm clubs as a place to assess individual accomplishments, the Orioles felt that a culture of winning started in the minors. The annoyed rumblings that I heard when I got sent to Rochester confirmed that this was true. "Why is Jim Palmer having spring training in Rochester when we're trying to win?" people asked. They meant business in Rochester.

After a month in Miami, I was summoned back to Baltimore, where I pitched a total of nine innings in two games with eight days off between starts. I was effective, however, which gave me hope that I would be my old self again after an offseason of rest. With sports medicine still in its infancy and MRIs a technology of the future, nobody in the Orioles organization had the ability to identify what was wrong with me. At one point, the Orioles sent me to a dentist to have a tooth pulled, thinking that a decaying molar might be responsible for my arm troubles. When that didn't work, a throat doctor removed my tonsils and adenoids on the theory that infections in those tissues had spread to the rest of my body. Not surprisingly, those procedures did nothing to help my aching shoulder. There was a knowledge gap back then. Doctors simply didn't know enough about athlete-specific injuries to give proper diagnoses. And old-school managers and coaches who kept themselves fit in the offseason by chopping wood or tilling fields just couldn't understand why a young player's body would break down like mine had. It was without a doubt one of the darkest and most frustrating periods in my life. I had to bite on a towel to keep from crying in pain. And as if the physical pain wasn't bad enough, I also had to deal with the emotional anguish of looking into an uncertain future.

I had every intention of getting past my problems and pitching effectively again, but the dawning of a new spring didn't bring restored health. My arm still felt terrible to the point where I had to be scratched from spring training starts. I had grown fed up with the whole situation. After testing my arm out one afternoon only to find that it felt no better, I chucked a ball against the outfield wall in frustration. It was my hardest delivery of spring training, according to Lou Hatter, the Orioles beat writer for *The Baltimore Sun*.

Another day, another trip to the doctor's office. But this time I visited a physician who found a way to give me temporary relief. In his role as team doctor for the Los Angeles Dodgers, Robert Kerlan had helped Sandy Koufax cope with his chronic arthritis problems. Along with his medical partner, Frank Jobe, Kerlan was a pioneer in the field of sports orthopedics. In addition to Koufax, Kerlan would go on to treat athletes ranging from jockey Willie Shoemaker to basketball star Kareem Abdul-Jabbar. Whereas other doctors were orthopedists who happened to treat athletes, Kerlan specialized in sports-related injuries. I traveled to Los Angeles and spent almost all of April in his care. After a month of rehabilitation with him, my shoulder felt better than it had in a very long time.

In Single A Miami to start the '68 season, I made two starts and didn't give up an earned run. Then it was back to Rochester, where I got hit hard in an exhibition game against the big league club, and eventually on to Double A Elmira, which brought me a step closer to making a complete tour of the Orioles minor league system, a rare journey for someone who already had a World Series win under his belt.

Bauer and his pitching coach, George Bamberger, expressed optimism about my chances of joining the Orioles starting rotation before the end of the '68 season. Up until that point, I, too, maintained faith that I somehow, some way would get better, that my body would heal, and that I'd pitch again in the major leagues. But the delivery of a single pitch in the minors in 1968 went a long way toward making me think my career was over. During a start for Elmira in Pittsfield, Massachusetts, I got ahead of Billy Conigliaro by throwing two fastballs for strikes. Thinking I'd try and blow another pitch by him, I reared back and threw another heater. As the ball left my hand, I heard something pop in my right shoulder area. My arm went limp. I stepped off the mound, realizing that I wouldn't be able to roll a ball to home plate—let alone throw one.

That was the last pitch I threw for Elmira or any other team during the regular season. The next day I flew back to Baltimore for examination. I was in the Orioles clubhouse with my shirt off when I got the news that no one—let alone any pitcher—ever wants to hear. Our assistant trainer, Ralph Salvon, who would soon be promoted to head trainer, broke it to me. "Jim," he said, "you have a big hole in your back." And that's how I found out I tore my rotator cuff.

In later years 1968 became famous as "the year of the pitcher." It was the season that Bob Gibson of the St. Louis Cardinals posted a remarkable 1.12 ERA and Denny McClain of the Detroit Tigers won an astounding 31 games. As these historic performances played out around the majors, I could only sit idly by and watch. I never felt more helpless. You can't win if you're not in the game, and I was starting to think that I might never experience the thrill of standing on a major league pitching mound again.

After finding out that I had a gaping hole in my back, I went to see Dr. Stanley Cohen at Sinai Hospital in Baltimore. He ran some tests on my shoulder area and found no nerve response in one of the rotator cuff muscles. To my ears that sounded bad... really bad. But Dr. Cohen assured me that it was possible for the nerves to regenerate and for the muscle to build back up. Again, back then, doctors were still developing an understanding of elbow and shoulder injuries, a process that would lead to the proliferation of Tommy John and rotator cuff surgeries. In 1968 I went the more traditional route, spending the next several weeks after my injury lifting weights in the hope that I could repair the damaged muscle on my own. I talked earlier about the elbow injury that prematurely ended Koufax's career. A few years later, Don Drysdale suffered the same fate due to a rotator cuff tear. Baseball careers are fragile. Koufax and Drysdale had great runs before bowing out due to injury. Many more pitchers experience career-ending injuries before they even have a chance to show what they can do, and in 1968 I was at serious risk of becoming one of them.

With all the uncertainty about my physical state, I felt very skittish about my future. I realized I couldn't just sit around and hope that everything would return to normal for me. I had a mortgage to pay and a wife and baby daughter to support. The situation caused me a lot of angst mainly because it made me confront the fact that I didn't have complete control over my fate. If you want to be a better basketball player, you work on your jump shot, free throws, and conditioning. If you want to get better grades, you ask questions and study more. You commit yourself to getting better. When you're a pitcher with a hurt arm, you're at the mercy of the healing process.

I never really had a Plan B in life. I always knew I wanted to be a baseball player and I was fortunate enough to fulfill that dream. But after I tore my rotator cuff, I realized I needed to explore other options. So I enrolled in classes at Towson State University, which was conveniently located near the YMCA where I worked out during my rehabilitation. I also took and passed an exam that made me a licensed life insurance salesman. I hoped I would never have to put the license to use. My mind raced as I tried to think of ways that I could remain involved in the game I loved even if I couldn't pitch anymore. It didn't seem likely that a major league team would be in the market for a 22-year-old coach, but maybe a college or high school might consider giving me a shot. Then there was the possibility of trying to convert myself into a position player. I wasn't a bad hitter. In fact I hit a home run in my first major league game. The legendary Billy Martin, while scouting for the Twins in 1964, had shown interest in signing me as an outfielder. If that had happened, baseball fans would have gotten to see me wear glasses. I never had to wear them while pitching, but if I was out shagging fly balls, I would have definitely needed them.

The baseball writers had started referring to me as "former Orioles right-hander" Jim Palmer. They were only half-joking. I didn't make a single appearance in the majors in 1968 and had been healthy enough to throw just 37 innings in the minors. I didn't know if I'd ever be well enough to pitch again. The writers had similar doubts and so too did Orioles management. In September 1968, as the team was finishing up a 91-win season, which was good enough for second in the American League, the Orioles placed me on waivers. I went unclaimed. A month later I became available again—this time to the American League expansion teams in Seattle and Kansas City. I wasn't one of the 60 players picked in the expansion draft. The Royals selected my teammate, right-handed pitcher Roger Nelson, as the first overall pick. In picking Nelson the Royals were going with the hot hand. After joining the Orioles starting rotation at the end of the '68 season, he had pitched extremely well. Unfortunately for Kansas City, he would go on to win just 25 more games the rest of his career.

Having missed most of the past two seasons, I knew I had a lot of hard work in front of me. The 1966 World Series seemed like ancient history. It felt like I was starting over. So rather than returning home for the offseason, I reported to the Florida Winter Instructional League, where I wasted no time in giving up 10 runs and 14 hits in a game. My arm didn't hurt anymore, but I had no velocity. The team I pitched against had Al Oliver, Bob Robertson, Manny Sanguillen, and several other guys I would go on to face in the '71 World Series. Our left fielder Terry Crowley must have shed 10 to 15 pounds running balls down in the outfield. I had to apologize to him between innings.

In a last-ditch effort to see if I could still pitch, the Orioles suggested I go to the Puerto Rican League to work with Bamberger. I was reluctant to go. Bamberger urged me to give it another month before I gave up hope of ever pitching well again. Prior to heading to San Juan, I attended a Baltimore Bullets basketball game at the Civic Center with a friend of mine named Marv Foxman, who worked for Eli Lilly and Company. Marv listened patiently as I told him all about my long struggle with arm and shoulder problems. I confessed that I thought my career was over. He listened to my litany of complaints and asked me if I had ever taken an anti-inflammatory drug called Indocin. He had samples in the car and offered to run out and get them at halftime. At this point I had nothing to lose. I took him up on his offer, procured a prescription, and hoped for the best.

For the first month in Puerto Rico, I threw on the side, waiting for the opportunity to test my arm in game situations. All the while

I took the anti-inflammatory that Marv told me about. It helped me immensely. In my first side session in front of Bamberger and Orioles head scout Walter Youse, I was able to throw 96 miles per hour without any pain. It was like I had a new arm. Playing for the Santurce Crabbers alongside teammates including Dave Leonhard, Elrod Hendricks, Jim Hardin, and Dave May, I went 6–1 and threw a seven-inning no-hitter. Frank Robinson, who had an eye on managing after his playing career ended, tried his hand at the job in Puerto Rico and was named the league's Manager of the Year.

My time in Puerto Rico gave me hope. For added inspiration I looked to my teammate, McNally, who after missing most of the 1967 season with arm problems, returned to win 22 games in 1968. If he could do it, why couldn't I? But if I hoped to get my career back on track, I needed to make adjustments, most notably by diversifying my pitch repertoire. In Puerto Rico I worked on improving my curveball and change-up. And the results were favorable. Amid all of the physical, mental, and emotional anguish that stems from not being able blow hitters away with fastballs, I learned how to pitch.

I was more motivated than ever to get my career back on track. But I had my work cut out for me. The Orioles were no longer reserving a spot for me in the starting rotation. Heck, I wasn't even guaranteed a spot on their Opening Day roster. The team cut my salary from $15,000 to $13,500, which I believe was the maximum allowable pay cut back then and certainly a sign that I had to go out and prove myself all over again. At the age of 23, when most players are still trying to make the majors, I had to claw my way back. And that meant impressing Earl Weaver, who took over as Orioles manager during the 1968 season.

At spring training in 1969, Earl said publicly that he had questions about my health. He wondered aloud whether the Jim Palmer who reported to camp was the same Jim Palmer who tossed a shutout in the '66 World Series. Earl was speaking for everyone in the organization when he voiced those concerns. When three days passed without my arm breaking down again, Earl was ecstatic. Bamberger told reporters that he liked what he saw from me in intra-squad scrimmages. My teammates also voiced support. My body was feeling good. And the positive reinforcement from my coaches and teammates helped get my head back in the right place.

As he prepared for his first full year as a big league manager, Earl's personality and motivational tactics started to shine through. Replacing Bauer as manager in Baltimore was his reward for managing some very successful teams in the Orioles' minor league system. And he wanted to show everyone who was boss.

We had a young pitcher at the time named Mike Adamson, a California kid who was a first-round draft pick out of USC in 1967. Since the amateur draft was instituted in 1965, only 21 players have gone straight to the major leagues without spending a day in the minors. Adamson was the charter member of that group. He made his debut with the Orioles less than a week after he agreed to terms on a contract that included a $100,000 signing bonus. I was really impressed by his raw ability, but in retrospect he probably could have benefitted from some time on the farm before making the leap to the majors.

In his second ever start for the Orioles, Adamson got into a first-inning jam in Boston. With a runner on base and one out, he faced Tony Conigliaro (older brother of Billy), who had emerged as one the best power hitters in the game. Adamson threw his first two pitches (both high fastballs) for strikes. Our catcher, Andy Etchebarren, called for a breaking pitch, but Adamson shook off the sign, prompting Andy to go out to the mound for a chat. "What do you want to do?" Andy asked.

"*What do I want to do?*" Adamson repeated in disbelief. "He can't hit my high fastball."

So Adamson came again with the high heat. Conigliaro made contact this time, and the ball soared out toward the Citgo sign beyond the Green Monster in left field. Adamson didn't pitch in another game in the majors that season. Demoted to Triple A, he performed well enough for the remainder of the '67 season and the first half of the next season to convince the Orioles to call him up after the All-Star break in 1968. His second shot in the majors went even worse than his first. After two horrendous starts, he got shipped back to Rochester.

By 1969 it looked like Adamson had finally figured out what he needed to do to make it in the major leagues. He threw really well at spring training, and as Opening Day neared, I felt like I might be competing with him for the final spot in the Orioles starting rotation. In late March before an exhibition game against the Washington Senators, Earl told Adamson that he was penciled in to pitch the final two innings in relief of me. Earl knew that Adamson understood what was riding on the final spring training games, so he tried to up the ante with him. Earl told him that if he pitched poorly against the Senators that he would be boarding a bus after the game and heading 250 miles north to Daytona Beach, where our Triple A team trained. Earl didn't say what would happen if Adamson pitched well. That was just Earl.

I pitched seven innings of two-run ball that day, and Adamson came in and tossed two perfect innings in relief. Earl admitted after the game that the threat of demotion to Rochester was a motivational ploy. Adamson made the Opening Day roster but didn't pitch effectively at all. By early May he was back in Rochester yet again. He never made it back to the majors, retiring from the game at the age of 21. According to Etchebarren, Adamson was never the same mentally after yielding the home run to Conigliaro in 1967. Our careers had an interesting parallel. A pitch I threw to Billy Conigliaro easily could have been my last. And a pitch that Adamson threw to Tony Conigliaro was symbolically his last, proving once again that baseball is as much mental as physical.

At times Earl fancied himself an amateur psychologist, but he also knew when to just come out and say what he meant. Near the end of spring training, he told reporters that I looked like I was on the comeback trail and that he expected big things from me. He felt I could be a key contributor to a team that he hoped would compete for a pennant. With four new expansion teams opening play in 1969, Major League Baseball broke with tradition and created two divisions in each league, meaning that instead of competing to beat out nine other teams to earn a trip to the World Series, we had to best five teams in our division to advance to the first ever American League Championship Series.

I accomplished my goals at spring training, pitching well enough not only to start the season in Baltimore but to earn a spot in the Orioles' five-man rotation. Six days into the 1969 season, I made my first major league appearance in more than 18 months, starting the first game of a doubleheader against the Senators. I walked the first batter of the game but then settled down and struck out the next three Senators. My confidence surged. From the first inning on, all my pitches were working. And I felt an ease on the mound that had eluded me through all my physical difficulties. I went the distance that day, throwing a five-hit shutout. Eight days later I blanked the Cleveland Indians on four hits.

By the end of June, I had a record of 9–2 and an ERA of 1.96. My strong first half of the season mirrored the team's remarkable start. On July 1 we stood 33 *games* above .500 and held an 11-game lead over the second-place Red Sox. Whatever Earl was doing seemed to be working. A back problem interrupted what was turning out to be a dream season, landing me on the disabled list in July. When I returned to the active roster in early August, we had further strengthened our grip on first place.

In my second start back, I experienced another early career highlight when I threw a no-hitter at Memorial Stadium against the Oakland A's. It wasn't the prettiest of no-nos. I walked the bases loaded in the ninth inning and yielded six free passes on the night. But it still felt great, especially because I accomplished the feat in front of our home crowd. I had pitched no-hitters in Aberdeen, South Dakota, and Santurce, Puerto Rico, but the one at Memorial Stadium carried with it a special thrill. While we celebrated my big night in the clubhouse, Frank Robinson, the judge of our team's kangaroo court, fined me for a base-running blunder I had committed. I was more than happy to pay. The no-hitter turned out to be the first of five consecutive complete games for me.

We got tremendous starting pitching in 1969. Mike Cuellar, whom we acquired from the Houston Astros prior to the season, won 23 games. McNally won 20 games, including his first 15 decisions in a row, the longest such streak to start a season. I finished 16–4 and likely would have joined the 20-win club if I hadn't missed six weeks of the season. At the plate we scored more runs than any other American League team. On the final day of the regular season, I pitched a 10-inning complete game against the Detroit Tigers, helping us to register our 109th win of the season, the most ever in franchise history. We left every other American League East team in the dust and went on to sweep the Twins in the best-of-five American League Championship Series. In what was another special moment in my comeback season, I was standing on the mound when we clinched our second trip to the World Series in four years.

Unlike in the 1966 Fall Classic, when we entered as heavy underdogs against Koufax, Drysdale, and the Dodgers, most people expected us to have an easy time with the upstart Mets. Nobody thought "the other New York team" had a chance of getting as far as they had, and had it not been for an incredible stretch run and a total collapse by the Chicago Cubs, they wouldn't have made the postseason. With the exception of Tom Seaver, who won a career-high 25 games in '69, they lacked real star power. But teams don't win 100 regular season games by accident. And I think a lot of people forget that the '69 Mets won that many games. The Mets, who had been the laughingstock of baseball since becoming a franchise in 1962, were playing with fire in their bellies after sweeping the Atlanta Braves in the National League Championship Series, and they believed they could beat anybody, including the heavily favored Orioles.

The "Amazin' Mets" earned their nickname against us. After we took the first game at home against Seaver, the Mets rattled off four straight victories to win it all. I didn't help our cause, losing Game 3 at Shea Stadium. Pitching on eight days' rest, I struggled to control my curveball, which in turn meant the Mets knew to look for my fastball. For those who remember, it was the Tommie Agee game. Agee led off the bottom of the first with a home run, one of only two leadoff homers I surrendered in my career. (The other time was in the 1977 All-Star Game when Joe Morgan led off the game with a homer into the right-field stands.) Later in the game, Agee made a couple of spectacular plays in the field that saved several runs.

By Game 4 I think everyone saw the direction the series was going. Earl definitely did and he went down fighting, becoming the first manager in decades to get ejected from a World Series game for arguing balls and strikes with home plate umpire Shag Crawford.

Ralph Waldo Emerson said, "Life is a journey, not a destination," and the journey to my second World Series felt incredible. We simply ran into a Mets team that refused to fall short of its goal. With the benefit of time, I can see that the Miracle Mets were a great underdog story, and their victory created an iconic moment for baseball. I don't think we underestimated them. They deserved to win. That doesn't mean that I'm completely over the loss. In 1999 at the annual Baseball Assistance Team's fundraiser in New York, several former Mets and Orioles got together to celebrate/lament the 30th anniversary of the '69 World Series. Broadcaster Gary Thorne, the emcee of the event, asked Seaver and me about our memories of the series. I told him that I don't think much about it anymore, but when they broadcast any of the games on ESPN Classic, I walk right out of the room. Seaver laughed and said, "Jim, it was 30 years ago. You have to let it go."

Rather than dwelling on coming up short in the '69 World Series, I prefer to focus on the perseverance and hard work that allowed me to get there in the first place. You can't truly appreciate the feeling of being on top until you've experienced what it's like at the bottom. In January of 1969, I couldn't have said for sure if I would pitch again in the major leagues. And if I did, I had no idea if I would ever match the level of success that I experienced in my first full season. Ten months and 16 wins later, I got a chance to pitch in my second World Series. Despite losing the '69 World Series, we had a lot to look forward to in the coming years. The Orioles organization had built a foundation of greatness that would lead to the most fulfilling years of my life.

No one wants to experience adversity, but we all do at one time or another. It's inevitable. The question is not *if* we'll face obstacles, it's how we'll conquer and learn from them. Don't get me wrong, I wish I hadn't lost nearly two years of my career to injury. But in the long run, I think the entire experience benefitted me. It helped me gain valuable perspective and put me in touch with a competitive spirit that I didn't know I had. Up until my arm injury, things had come naturally for me. After my injury I had to learn to get by with less. The one-hitter I threw against the Yankees in 1967 is a good example of that.

No one goes through their professional life without experiencing obstacles and adversity. When you're in the midst of hard times, your focus is on righting the ship. That's a given. Once you've overcome a setback, however, you have a valuable opportunity to make yourself better and more successful moving forward.

VISIT TO THE MOUND

The seasons covered in this chapter were without a doubt the most difficult of my career. But they were also the most pivotal. Between the ages of 20 and 22, I went from the euphoria of playing in a World Series to the despair of suffering a career-threatening injury and back again. It was a journey that paved the way for everything that would come later. And it taught me a lot of lessons that I think are worth sharing.

For the purposes of this discussion, we'll assume that the workplace woes that afflict most people aren't related to sickness or injury. We all get into ruts in our professional lives that affect our output or the quality of work that we do. In the beginning my problem was purely physical, but after a while, my inability to do my job effectively resulted in significant mental and emotional stress. I'm sure many of you have been in the same position. If you believe in yourself and the goal you're trying to accomplish in the workplace, you can overcome these barriers. It comes down to having the proper mind-set and attitude. First and foremost, that means avoiding the tendency to take criticism too personally. How do you deal with adversity? By getting frustrated and making excuses or by working harder and re-examining your approach? Do you brainstorm ideas and solutions or do you give up, pack up, and go home? Be aware of your default pattern because, typically, how you do one thing is how you do everything.

It's natural to feel hurt when we get negative feedback from those who evaluate us, and I won't pretend to think that such criticism never has a personal component to it. But if you stay focused on the work, you're in a better position to succeed.

It was humbling for me to get crushed by minor league hitters in 1967 and 1968. But I stayed focused on what I needed to do to get back on top. That brings me to my second point: I wouldn't have been able to mount a successful comeback if I didn't develop new skills. I was never going to be the fastball pitcher that I was before my injuries. So I developed into more of a control pitcher by learning to locate my pitches better. We can all benefit from learning new skills. Especially in a world of incredible technological advances, we can feel more secure and be more successful in the workplace by expanding our repertoire.

It's important to remember that we're humans, not machines. We feel pain and anguish, sometimes so acutely that we don't know how we'll go on. And that's okay. There's nothing wrong with showing fear. We can't confront our emotions until we recognize them.

In sports we hear a lot about the importance of "grit." A lot of times, the word is used to describe an undersized athlete who works hard and "plays the game the right way." But it's much broader and more universal than that. Angela Lee Duckworth, a psychology professor at the University of Pennsylvania, has spent a lot of time looking at the qualities that make people successful. At a Technology, Entertainment, Design (TED) Talk, Duckworth explained: "One characteristic emerged as a significant predictor of success. And it wasn't social intelligence. It wasn't good looks or physical health. And it wasn't IQ. It was grit. Grit is passion and perseverance for very long-term goals. Grit is having stamina. Grit is sticking with your future, day in and day out, not just for a week, not just for a month, but for years and working really hard to make that future a reality. Grit is living life like it's a marathon, not a sprint."

Articulate your "marathon" goal. Share your goals with your friends and family to create accountability. If you don't know what you want and where you want to go and most importantly, why you want it, it's a heck of a lot harder to get there. We all stumble at some point during the race of life, but we have to remember that we're running a marathon and always have time to regain our footing.

4TH INNING

Building Trust

I HAD AN ATYPICAL UPBRINGING, AND MY CHILDHOOD and adolescence went a long way toward shaping the person I later became. The environment I grew up in heavily influenced my outlook on life, especially with regards to my belief that strong relationships are one of the foundations of success.

Before I was Jim Palmer, I was Jim Wiesen, the adopted son of Moe and Polly Wiesen, a New York City couple who brought me into their home when I was just two days old. My adoptive mom was born and raised in Omaha, Nebraska, the daughter of a Union Pacific Railroad worker who died of a heart attack in his early 40s. A few years after his death, she left the heartland for the Big Apple, where she helped put her brother, Bob, through Juilliard School of Music by working in a dress shop. At work she met and fell in love with my adoptive father, a garment industry executive. After getting married they adopted a little girl named Bonnie and shortly thereafter they added me to their family. My dad was Jewish, my mom was Catholic with leanings toward Christian Science, and I somehow grew up Presbyterian.

My father owned two dress companies and had his office at 1400 Broadway, the mecca of the garment industry. With my parents away from home a lot of the time, a couple named George and Ruth came to our Park Avenue apartment to look after my sister and me. During the school year, I spent more time with George and Ruth than my parents. And in the summer, I went away to Camp Half Moon in Great Barrington, Massachusetts.

The many tasks George performed included playing catch with me in the courtyard of our building. My interest in baseball blossomed at an early age, a process aided and abetted by watching the great New York Yankees teams of the era. I remember rushing home from school when I was seven years old to watch Game 7 of the 1952 World Series between the Yankees and Brooklyn Dodgers. Billy Martin made a great catch in the seventh inning of that game, helping the Yankees win their fourth of five World Series in a row.

The first decade of my life could have passed for a 1950s period piece. There's a fabulous family photo from the Park Avenue days of my dad in a sharp charcoal gray suit, my mom in a swing dress with a drink and a cigarette in her hand, and me in a little suit and bow tie. We looked like Don Draper and his family from the TV show *Mad Men*.

I was about eight years old when I learned I had been adopted. My grandmother told me on a Saturday morning. I don't remember the details of the conversation—only that it was the first time that I had ever heard the word. After Nana explained it to me, I still didn't really understand what it meant. I had always felt loved, so it didn't really matter to me how my parents became my parents. I couldn't have been more fortunate.

Looking back on it, that conversation with my grandmother likely was prompted by my father's failing health. It took place around the time we moved to a house in suburban Harrison, New York, where my father remained confined to the first floor, as his heart was too weak to climb stairs. Eventually, he had a house built in Rye, New York. But he still went into work. And he made Saturdays our father-son days. He'd go over some numbers at his Broadway office, and then we'd have lunch and go shopping.

On one such Saturday in 1955, I woke up, looked out the window, and saw a number of cars in the driveway. I went downstairs to see what was going on. My mom told me that my father had died of heart failure.

I was old enough to understand the meaning of death but too young to fully grasp its consequences. My father was gone and not coming back—that much I knew. The aftermath of that morning, the grieving, the funeral, etc., was a blur. I know my mom was grieving. She and my father had built a life and business together in New York.

And after his death, his business partners sold off many of the assets, leaving my mother in a position where she could go anywhere she pleased. I don't think New York would have ever been the same for her without my father, so she opted for a radical change of scene. My father had helped her brother, Bob, move out to Whittier, California, and open three dress stores. She decided that we might all benefit from a fresh start on the West Coast, so we went out to join Bob.

A decade in the New York City area had left my mother with an appreciation for big-city amenities. After about a year in Whittier, she yearned for a more cosmopolitan experience and moved us 30 miles toward the coast to Beverly Hills. An avid golfer, she found herself in a foursome one day with a man named Max. They got along well and arranged to play another round of golf the following week. After that they started seeing each other on a regular basis. I liked Max a lot. When he went out with my mom, he would include me, even if it meant watching movies he didn't necessarily want to see or eating at restaurants he wouldn't have picked. Speaking of movies, Max was an actor—not a movie star but a character actor—who appeared in several popular television shows of the 1950s, including *Dragnet*, *Route 66*, and a series called *Gangbusters*, in which he played a character named Schafer, who killed three people in the course of a half-hour episode. I still have the tape in my collection. That's what you call acting because in real life Max was a real gentle and loving guy. He couldn't support himself (or a family) solely on the acting gigs, so he supplemented his income by working as a bar manager at Santa Anita and Hollywood parks.

When I was 12, my mom told me that she and Max planned to get married. She said that she would be taking his name and that it would make him happy and proud if I did the same. That's a big decision for a kid, and I told her that I would have to think about it. A few months after the wedding, we attended a Little League awards dinner, where I was picking up three trophies—two for hitting and one for playing on the championship team. I decided it was the perfect opportunity to grant Max's wish. I told the coaches who were presenting the awards that I wanted to be introduced by my new name, "Jim Palmer." Max cried three times that night and in the years that followed he often said that what transpired at the Little League banquet had more meaning to him than anything I later accomplished in my major league career. Max was a wonderful man and a wonderful stepfather.

My life really took off after I moved out to California and started playing organized baseball. The clearest and fondest memories of my childhood involve hitting and throwing a baseball. An old photo that Max and my mom kept in our living room shows me playing in the Beverly Hills Little League wearing high-top sneakers because the sporting goods stores didn't have cleats big enough for me. Once I got into sports, everything else fell into place. They gave my life structure and meaning. My parents always emphasized the importance of getting good grades, and I obliged by making sure my schoolwork never suffered. But my real passion was sports. I developed a happy routine: go to school, come home and do my paper route (delivering the *Beverly Hills Independent*), and then play baseball, basketball, or football until it was time for dinner and homework.

During high school my family moved to Scottsdale, Arizona. I loved baseball but decided not to limit myself to just one sport at Scottsdale High School. By my senior year, I had earned all-state honors in baseball, football, and basketball. I think I benefitted from not specializing in baseball. Participating in several sports taught me the value of honing different skillsets, as well as how to thrive in various team settings. Spring and summer belonged to baseball, but running pass routes in the fall and grabbing rebounds in the winter left me with a lot of cherished memories. I wish more kids today opted against focusing all their energies on a single sport. You're only young once, and adolescence is an ideal time to try out different experiences.

Throughout high school I dated a young woman named Susan Ryan. To earn a few bucks to take her out on weekends, I'd mow our yard and clean our pool, sometimes in the 115-degree Arizona heat. I developed some really good friendships in Scottsdale, including with

Frank "Dusty" Blethen, who went on to become the publisher of *The Seattle Times*. I knew what my parents' expectations were of me and in most cases I met or exceeded them. It's a lot easier to follow rules when they are clearly articulated to you. And I felt my parents' rules were fair. That helped us avoid the pitfalls of so many teenager-parent relationships. Max and my mom trusted me. Sometimes I'd bend that trust by sneaking out of the house at night to cruise around with my friends. When we got back home, my friends and I would try to tiptoe into the house undetected. One of those times at around 2:00 AM, we saw a light go on in the kitchen. Then the back door swung open. It was Max. We braced ourselves for a scolding, but instead we were met with a question: "You boys want a sandwich?" We went into the kitchen and ate a post-midnight snack with Max.

On the subject of sandwiches, Max loved to tell the story about my Sunday night routine of laying five slices of white bread on the kitchen counter, placing a slice of bologna on each, topping them all with another slice of bread, sliding the five bologna sandwiches into little plastic bags, and putting the baggies in the refrigerator. I stayed very busy from Monday through Friday and by following these simple steps I could make lunch for the entire week.

I worked hard to nurture the athletic gifts that had been bestowed upon me. When I came home from whatever practice I was attending, I'd help with dinner, clean the dishes, do my home-work, and wrap up my day by going out and shooting some baskets or running a couple of miles. Am I a Type A personality? Yes, I am and I always have been. Time and again, people have accused me of being a perfectionist, as if the word carries a negative connotation. I've never understood that. Should we make it our goal to be aver-age? Why would anybody do that? You work as hard as you do to separate yourself from the pack.

My biggest weakness in high school was my shyness. I loved playing sports but dreaded having to speak publicly about anything I accomplished on the field or court. As captain of the football and basketball teams, I occasionally had to say a few words to the entire student body at pep rallies. Those awkward speeches never failed to ruin my day. Another time in high school, a friend who was running for class president asked me to endorse his candidacy at a school assembly. I agreed to introduce him and say a few nice things about him in front of our peers. It didn't go well. The moment I got up on stage, every muscle in my body tensed up, including the ones that controlled speech. I probably dashed any chances my friend had of getting elected to that or any other post. I just didn't feel comfortable as a public speaker, a shortcoming I would later confront head-on.

I was offered a scholarship my senior year to play basketball for John Wooden at UCLA but instead chose to sign with the Orioles. At the outset of my professional baseball career, I married Susan. We had two daughters together before splitting up after 20 years of marriage. I remarried several years later only to get divorced again. Since 2007 I've been married to my lovely wife, who is also named Susan.

While my mother and Max took great joy in watching my baseball career blossom, my sister, Bonnie, and I grew apart after we reached adulthood. I haven't heard from her in 25 years. She's lived a transient life and has been married five or six times. Though we grew up in the same households, we developed into very different people. It happens, I guess.

As for my birth parents, I never felt the impulse to contact them or even to find out who they were. They never approached me either. Somewhere, I have my birth certificate, which lists my mother's last name as "Maroney." That's where my knowledge of her begins and ends. I didn't need to know more. That might seem unusual, especially to other adoptees, many of whom decide at some point in their lives to pursue a relationship with their "bio moms."

In a 2011 essay for *Psychology Today* titled "Why Adoptees Need to Find Their Biological Parents," Stephen J. Bechten, himself an adoptee, explained why he chose to track down his birth mother after he was well into adulthood. "By the time I hit my 40s, I was tired of the intrigue," he wrote. "My adopted parents were deceased, and I felt it was time to explore what I came to see as a hole in my life. The research indicates that many adopted children feel this way and may embark on a biological search even if they've had a positive experience with their adopted parents." Bechten established a temporary relationship with the woman who brought him into the world and felt better off for doing so.

Lisa Lutz, writing in *The New York Times Magazine* in 2012, shared a different experience. She called her essay, "I Found My Biological Parents, and I Wish I Hadn't." Lutz took the plunge at 37. Her brief time with her birth father concluded with him asking her if she wanted him to take her to Disneyland.

Long story short, there's no right answer. All we can hope for is that we grow up and always live in loving environments. I definitely did. In the 1980s I appeared on Sally Jessy Raphael's talk show alongside other famous adoptees, including Wendy's founder Dave Thomas and CBS anchorwoman Faith Daniels. The topic had particular meaning to Sally, who herself was adopted.

You don't have to be a biological parent to be a good parent. I'm still learning that at the age of 70 as the stepfather to an autistic young man named Spencer. He's a lovable kid who brings Susan and me a lot of joy. But it can be challenging to raise a special-needs child. The traditional parent-child relationship shifts in some really significant ways. In all cases you try to give your children a foundation of principles that you hope will benefit them later in life. You nurture them and when the time is right you move on from them and let them experience all that comes their way. With special-needs children you do the same thing but with much less certainty about where life's path will take them. It can be frightening.

Spencer has a photographic memory. He devours movies and communicates largely through them. That's how you start conversations with him. He loves the Indiana Jones movies so much that we've nicknamed him "Indy." He's also a creature of habit. For example, we rarely turn the air conditioning on in our Orange County, California, home because the weather is usually perfect without much humidity. But if on a muggy day the air kicks on automatically, Spencer, unnerved by the sound and the sensation of the blowing air, will immediately get up and turn the air off. When I drive him to school, I have to take the same route every day or risk an outburst. All of this is okay because I feel unconditional love for him.

From my early childhood in New York to my teenage years in California and Arizona, I always felt like I had a tremendous support network. As a husband and father, I have tried to give my family the same level of nurturing because there's no question that we take a lot of what we learn in our home environment out into the world with us.

You know that saying about how you can't choose your family? Well, the same applies to your co-workers and managers. And because many adult Americans spend the majority of their waking hours on the job, it's essential to understand how to navigate workplace dynamics. In baseball you spend entire summers surrounded by 24 male siblings and a substitute dad. Not surprisingly, the dynamics in this workplace family can get interesting, especially when the substitute dad is named Earl Weaver. But baseball teams aren't that different from other organizations. Some are healthy, functional, and successful, while others slip into a morass of personality conflicts, infighting, and sheer misery. "When playing out positively, there is a self-fulfilling virtuous cycle in which bosses help their employees develop and grow while employees reciprocate with achievements and contributions," wrote Ben Dattner, a workplace consultant, in *Psychology Today*. "Authority and power relationships in the workplace share some important psychological commonalities with parent-child relationships. Negative self-fulfilling cycles can occur when boss and employee expect and provide failure and criticism." Dattner also draws parallels between co-worker and sibling relationships: "Sibling relationships, in which there is a delicate balance between cooperation and competition, can serve as a model for one's relationships and interactions with one's peers."

I could fill an entire book with stories about the authority figure who became the biggest part of my workplace existence. In fact I did in a 1996 book I wrote called *Together We Were Eleven Foot Nine*, a work that includes almost every Earl Weaver anecdote I could remember. For the purposes of this book, I want to focus more on the stories that shed light on the way Earl exercised authority and viewed leadership and how his charges reacted to his style and methods.

The first point to emphasize is that Earl was more than just a ticking time bomb who strung together colorful streams of profanity and kicked dirt on umpires. For all his eccentricities and shoot-from-the-hip tendencies, he adhered to a strict philosophy of getting the most out of his players and putting individual and team success above all else. To his credit, on the rare occasions that he deviated from that philosophy, he acknowledged it.

> To build trust in yourself and others in your life, you must learn to put those around you first, meet the needs of others, and let your own needs follow. You must understand that your friends and employees are your most valuable assets. Once people realize that they are valued and part of something important, they will be more dedicated and committed to carrying out an organization's goals and missions.
>
> To get to this place, you must always keep your word, no matter what the cost. Keep conversations with friends and associates private. Don't embellish a fact or event to benefit yourself or to make yourself look good at the expense of others.
>
> Organizations that have lasting success take on a personality that is shaped by their leaders. You should maintain integrity across all areas of business and personal dealings with people and strive for a commitment to quality and honesty that will earn everyone's trust. I guess the Golden Rule tells it all: treat others as you would like them to treat you.
>
> Accountability helps build trust. No matter who you are, there is someone to whom you are accountable. Once you accept this fact, it will help you to be humble and willing to serve others in your relationships, which will help build trust. A relationship with God is a big part of my life, and I always remember to give thanks daily to the Lord for the talents and blessings He has given me. I am accountable to the Lord. He sets an example for me to follow.
>
> There will be trials, difficulties, troubles, and even failures in life. I have had my share of them. But out of them, you gain wisdom and become a stronger person, better equipped to serve others in your life.
> —DR. ROBERT HENDERSON, CHAIRMAN OF THE BOARD, NUTRAMAX LABORATORIES FAMILY OF COMPANIES

In late September 1969, Dave McNally was going for his 20th victory of the season against the Yankees. After winning his first 15 decisions before the All-Star break, he fell back to earth and had just a few starts left to reach the 20-win mark for the second consecutive season. Earl, too, was chasing a milestone. At 105–47 and with 10 games left to play, the Orioles had a shot at breaking the major league record of 111 wins in a season set by the 1954 Cleveland Indians. Never mind the fact that Cleveland reached that mark in a 154-game season, Earl wanted nothing more than to break the wins record in his first full year as manager. He never came right out and said it, but we all knew it. Though we had long ago clinched a spot in the postseason, Earl went about managing the final games of the season like they were crucial and meaningful contests.

McNally didn't have his best stuff that afternoon. We trailed 4–1 when we came to bat in the bottom of the fifth inning, and with a runner on first and nobody out, Earl opted to lift Dave for a pinch hitter. Dave, who had his helmet on and a bat in his hand and was ready to walk up to the plate, angrily confronted Earl about the decision. "I have a chance to win my 20th game, and you're pulling me? We can still come back and win this game."

"I have to think about the other 24 guys on the team," Weaver shot back. "Merv [Rettemund] is hitting for you."

Dave wasn't appeased. He darted back to the dugout, tore off the nylon batting jacket he was wearing, and slammed his helmet and bat to the ground. He then started the long march back to the home clubhouse. Without missing a beat, Earl scampered out of the dugout and gave chase. I didn't see what transpired next, but I heard all about it from Dave, who continued to tell Earl in private just how he felt. "How could you take me out?" he asked in amazement. "I'm going to pitch almost 300 innings this season, and it would be nice to have an opportunity to win my 20th game. But you're not going to give me that chance because all you're thinking about is yourself. You say you're thinking about the other 24 guys on the team, but that's not true. We've already won the division. You're thinking about yourself. And I just want you to know that."

In most situations Earl would have exploded, using every obscenity imaginable to tell Dave what he thought of his opinion. But apparently Dave's words resonated with him. Instead of firing off a retort, he just stood there, and his eyes slowly welled up with tears. When Dave and Earl came back to the dugout, we could tell Earl had been crying. It was an amazing sight. Earl's visceral reaction to Dave's criticism had deeper meaning. I think he realized that maintaining high morale among his players was essential to accomplishing his goals. For all of his tantrums and cutting one-liners, Earl intuitively knew that if he didn't reward his players for doing their jobs well, they might start lacking motivation. After it was too late to do anything about it, he realized that was justification enough to keep an ambitious pitcher in a game even when he didn't have his best stuff.

The story had a happy ending. We came back to beat the Yankees that day, and though Dave didn't get the win, he came back to notch his 20th in his next start. We, meanwhile, fell three wins short of breaking the Indians' record.

McNally and I formed a potent one-two punch on the mound in the late 1960s and early 1970s. We shared the same type of competitive spirit, but our contrasting approaches to dealing with Earl showed how differently our brains worked. I would engage Earl in conversation, trying to coax answers out of him and figure out what made him tick. I would ask questions and share my opinions on the subjects we discussed. The story I just related was noteworthy not only because it resulted in Earl shedding tears, but also because it was one of the rare occasions that Dave bothered to tell Earl what he really thought. Generally, Dave avoided saying much more than "yes" or "no" to Earl. The pitcher who said little and the one who said a lot developed a repartee that helped us and everyone else on the team deal with our manager's bluster.

You can't truly understand people until you know where they came from. Earl, who spent his late teenage years and all of his 20s fighting tooth and nail to make it to the major leagues, is no exception. When he signed with his hometown St. Louis Cardinals in

1948, the team assigned him a jersey with "521" on the back. In other words he had a lot of players he had to outplay if he ever hoped to don a uniform with a number in the single or double digits. But his resolve was stronger than most of his peers. He battled his way to the starting second baseman job for the Cardinals' lower minor league teams, progressing to the next level in each of his first three seasons. He liked to tell everybody how, despite hitting only two home runs, he led the league in RBIs one of those years. We joked that the only way he could have knocked in so many runs was by repeatedly coming up with the bases loaded and leaning into fastballs.

Earl never amounted to anything more than an above-average minor league player, but he liked to inflate his credentials when lecturing his team. During one particular meeting, he informed us that as a player he had never left a guy on third base with less than two outs, nor had he ever made the last out of a game. It would have been difficult to fact-check the statement, but considering Earl had more than 5,000 minor league plate appearances, it seemed unlikely that the boast had any merit. Instead of calling him out on his tall tale, we decided to take it at face value and have a little fun with it.

Dave was the first to chime in: "That's great, Earl, especially considering you never played higher than Double A." In reality, Earl had gotten a few at-bats at Triple A, but you could almost see the smoke coming from his ears.

Then it was my turn.

"You know why you never made the last out of a game?" I asked.

"Why's that?"

"Because they always pinch hit for you."

Earl had heard enough. "Okay, that's it! Meeting over!"

Quite possibly the greatest barb ever directed at Earl is often attributed to me, but it actually came from Dave on one of the many days that Earl stood with us in the outfield before a game and lectured us on how to pitch. Dave waited until Earl had finished his sermon before uttering the immortal words, "Earl, the only thing you know about pitching is that you couldn't hit it." It's a quote that I've been happy to modify and repeat many times over the years.

Earl valued winning above all else and devoted himself to doing as much of it as he could. He wasn't wired like most people. If we went on a 10-game winning streak but then lost our next game, he would react like we hadn't won a game in weeks. He had a short memory for our wins, but boy, did he remember all of our losses. And unlike the blow-ups he had with me and other players, which he quickly brushed aside and didn't hold grudges about, he took losses very personally. It was a good thing then that he had only one losing season in his managerial career. And it was no accident that that particular season ended up being his last.

An early spring training game we played in Mexico City in 1970 showed how much Earl hated to lose. He was on edge even before we boarded the flight to Mexico. We had lost only a total of five games the previous exhibition season, but already that spring, we had lost two. It didn't matter that we had won five. He was counting the losses and still reeling over having lost the '69 World Series to the New York Mets.

None of the players were real thrilled about making the trip south of the border. We finished playing a Sunday game and had to rush to the airport for our flight out. I didn't know if they'd even have time to wash our uniforms before we started the three-game Mexico City series the next day. At the Miami airport, I cracked a joke about aviation safety with my friend and teammate Davey Leonhard. Earl saw Davey and me fooling around in the boarding area and reamed us out. "If you don't want to make this trip, it'll cost you $100!" he yelled at Davey. He then turned to me with an enormous sneer on his face. "And if you don't want to go, it'll cost you $1,000!"

Earl's mood grew darker, when in the first game in Mexico, Pete Richert gave up a three-run home run in the bottom of the ninth inning, and we lost 8–7. In the clubhouse after the game, Earl redefined the meaning of the "Ugly American," hurling equipment and food around the locker room all because we had dropped our third spring training game. He was afraid we were getting complacent. That was Earl.

Earl and I had a lot more in common than some people may think. For one thing we shared a keen eye for the details of the game and both understood that individuals and teams that don't pay attention to the so-called small stuff could end up with large problems. Earl took it upon himself to squeeze every last ounce of potential out of his players, but sometimes I had to coax him into addressing certain issues that were driving me crazy.

Pat Kelly, a journeyman right fielder who joined our club in 1977, certainly wasn't the first baseball player who liked to party. But he discovered religion midway through his 15-year career. I didn't begrudge his faith. I just didn't think he should be espousing it during outfield practice before games, especially considering he could be a liability on defense. By the time he left the Orioles in 1980, he had succeeded in making several players born-again Christians. I was fine with that. Who my teammates prayed to was nobody's business but their own.

Eventually, Earl got wise to Kelly's overzealousness in preaching the gospel. On a beautiful July afternoon during the 1979 season, Pat hit a towering pinch-hit grand slam against the Oakland A's to give us a late-inning lead. Back in the dugout, he pointed to the heavens and exclaimed, "Thank you, Jesus! Thank you, Jesus!" As the rest of us were high-fiving each other, Pat was overcome with religious fervor. When Earl came over to congratulate him, he stopped and became reflective. "Earl, when are you going to walk with the Lord?" he asked.

"When you start walking with the bases loaded," Earl replied.

It was a great line, but even Earl would admit that a grand slam beats a bases-loaded walk any day.

Doug DeCinces' situation was comparable. But rather than strictly following the teachings of a god, he was trying to follow in the footsteps of one. DeCinces started seeing serious time at third base in 1975, the season that Brooks Robinson's Hall of Fame career started to go into rapid decline. DeCinces got off to a slow start at the plate that season, but considering Brooks' own recent problems at the dish, that wasn't what invited the scrutiny of fans and teammates. Nobody could play third base like Brooks, and every time

DeCinces booted a grounder, he would hear it from the fans. The booing shook his confidence so badly that he sought psychological counseling. I didn't expect DeCinces to be the next coming of Brooks Robinson, but I hoped he would devote himself to becoming the best third baseman he could and stop trying to backhand balls all the time. In retrospect, I should have been more sensitive to what it was like for Doug to succeed a legend like Brooks, but sometimes wisdom comes with age.

Sometime in the mid-1970s, I took Earl aside and made a plea for help. "There's a couple of things I want you to do, and then I won't say another word," I told him, hoping that he would agree to the first part and promptly forget the second. "First, tell Pat Kelly to work on his fielding and stop trying to convert people to Christianity in left field during batting practice because balls are falling in all over the place during games. And second, get Doug DeCinces to stop trying to backhand everything at third base."

I suppose I could have just held my tongue and pitched and let Earl handle personnel matters as he saw fit. But that wasn't my nature. I wanted my team to win and I just assumed that Earl would do everything in his power to help achieve that goal. So what was wrong with weighing in with a little constructive criticism from time to time?

We often find ourselves in delicate workplace situations. When is it appropriate to go to your boss with a critique of your co-workers? Is the possible good that can come out of such a conversation worth the potential strain it might cause to a relationship? I don't claim to know the answer to that question. It's a situational thing, I suppose. My input didn't always endear me to teammates. DeCinces called me out in *The Baltimore Sun*. He said, "Jim likes to air us out in the press. But when we do it, he can't take it." Like I said, I should have been more compassionate about what Doug was going through. To his credit, after getting off to a rocky start defensively, he developed into a better than average fielder and a solid all-around player who hit 237 career home runs, many of them with the California Angels.

He and I got past our initial conflict and developed a friendship that has lasted several decades.

You find all kinds of personality types in a baseball clubhouse or an office. Some guys I played alongside were real extroverts. Rick Dempsey may have been the biggest, but unlike me, he didn't turn his occasional disdain for Earl into a public spectacle. As the guy who caught most of my games from 1976 to 1984, he got stuck in the middle of a lot of disputes between Earl and me. Demper hated when we started yelling at each other during mound visits. Sometimes he'd put his mask back on and go chat with the home-plate umpire until we were finished cursing each other out. Other teammates, like Frank Robinson, went about their business quietly. But they had an unspoken understanding. Frank didn't say much to Earl, and Earl didn't say much to him. Not everybody loved each other, but I never played on a team that failed to reach its potential on the field because of personality conflicts off of it. Fortunately, we never had anybody who was clubhouse poison. Earl's oversized personality and unpredictable antics helped ensure that we players stuck together. Who had time to get angry with a teammate when Earl was acting as a constant irritant? If nothing else, we could always commiserate over Earl's latest outburst or collectively roll our eyes at one of his sermons. He antagonized all of us, reducing the need for us to antagonize each other. As Demper puts it, "Earl would always tell us we can't do this or can't do that, and we took real pleasure in going out and proving him wrong. We wanted to beat the opposition, but we also wanted to beat Earl Weaver."

Dave Leonhard, whom I roomed with in A ball and again for a few years in Baltimore, also has some pretty solid observations about Earl. And Davey is as equipped as anyone to weigh in on the subject because he took a psychology class in college. After playing for Earl at Double A, Triple A, and in the majors, he probably could have qualified for a PhD in psychology. Here's Davey's take on why Earl drove his players hard: "Earl felt that anybody who had a lot of talent and wasn't successful must not be prepared or working hard, or that he had some kind of flaw in his character. It pissed him off because he didn't have a lot of talent as a player, but he always tried as hard as he could."

So why was he so confrontational with me? I stayed in shape, prided myself on my high level of preparation, and committed myself to being the best I could. Well, I think he was suspicious of me for two reasons: my big mouth and my sometimes fragile body. I think he would have left me alone if I hadn't decided early on in our relationship to not give him the last word on every matter. I genuinely enjoyed verbally sparring with Earl and I'm sure he felt the same way. It allowed us to blow off steam and practice our one-liners, which served us both well in the broadcast booth after our time with the Orioles ended. I think it also drove Earl crazy that I wasn't made of iron or steel. He had a difficult time accepting that there were times in my career when I couldn't take the mound due to injury. He thought I was being a hypochondriac. And what Earl felt rubbed off on some of my teammates, who jokingly named the clubhouse whirlpool after me.

Some of Earl's quips about my injury history became the stuff of lore. For example, he once commented about how the Chinese tell time by the Year of the Dragon and the Year of the Horse, but that he tells time by my injuries: "The Year of the Shoulder, the Year of the Elbow, the Year of the Ulnar Nerve."

As profane and pointed as our arguments occasionally became, we never developed an actual dislike for each other. In fact, our relationship always maintained an element of affection. If Earl saw something he liked from me, he could be effusive with praise. He especially appreciated attention to detail. I remember a game in Boston when I pounced off the mound to field a sacrifice bunt attempt, wheeled around, and threw out the lead runner at second base to start a double play. "That was an exceptional play—so beautiful," Earl gushed after the game.

From a tactical standpoint, there were few managers better than Earl. Some managers reach the top of their profession because they're so exceptional at dealing with people and know how to inspire. Tommy Lasorda comes to mind. Tommy wasn't a master strategist, but he connected with his players on a human level. Earl was the opposite. He was a skilled in-game manager who did just enough off the field to prevent his players from rising up against him. There's a reason a book he wrote is called *Weaver on Strategy*—and not *Weaver on Being Nice to People*.

Earl's primary goal was to win, but he also liked to put on a show. Davey picked up on that early in Earl's managerial career when he played for him in the minors: "A couple of times at Rochester, I'd be sitting next to him in the dugout when a close play happened out on the field. He'd turn to me and say in a perfectly conversational tone, 'Watch this.' Then he'd run out on the field and go into one of his tantrums, spitting on the umpire, kicking dirt, uprooting a base and taking it into the dugout. It was just to entertain the fans and make it memorable for them."

Earl and I spent a lot of good years together, and I'll return to my relationship with him time and again in the pages that follow. He was the yin to my yang. And if you believed everything written in the newspaper about us, you'd think we absolutely loathed each other. But in reality our feelings for each other were far more complex. I didn't hate Earl, and he didn't hate me. It just seemed that way because we both had big mouths and squabbled publicly like an old married couple. I would tell Earl how to manage, and he would tell me how to pitch.

One story gets to the heart of several aspects of our multi-layered relationship. It starts with Earl's stubborn belief in my abilities, which never wavered in our many seasons together. In 1981 Ken Nigro of *The Sun* pointed out to Earl that opposing batters that season were hitting about .240 against me in innings one through six but over .400 in innings seven and beyond. That was a startling statistic, and it strongly implied that at the age of 35, I had lost some of my velocity. Most managers would have acted on this information by thinking twice about allowing me to pitch deep into games. Earl, however, wasn't most managers. He dismissed the notion that I was no longer able to throw 130 pitches in a game. Regardless of my age, I would always be the old Jim Palmer to Earl, who believed in me more than anybody I've known and loved the pitcher that I was at my peak. It broke his heart that, by 1981, I truly was the *older* Jim Palmer. Most managers would have grasped that reality and made concessions. Although I'm glad that I only wore an Orioles uniform for my entire career, one of the negatives of playing your entire career in one place is that it's hard for people to accept when you lose some of your skillset.

Earl must have thought that I put Nigro up to crunching those numbers because he became irate, accusing me of wanting to be pampered. It got tense between us, so much so that I temporarily moved my locker from next to Earl's office to the other side of the clubhouse. That pissed off Earl even more. Around this time he challenged me to a fight on the mound. Then he told Tom Boswell of *The Washington Post*, "I don't care if he dresses in the visitors' clubhouse. When I want him, I'll just send [pitching coach] Ray Miller over to drag him back by his diaper." Earl had a fixation with diapers. A couple of years earlier, he commented that umpire Steve Palermo "needs a diaper change" around the fifth inning of every game. In Earl's mind he was the only adult in a baseball world full of babies.

Earl gave the *Post* a million dollar quote, so of course Boswell came running to me for a response. By this point in my career, I had grown weary of the game of back and forth with Earl. "Tom, I know what you're looking for," I said. "You want some clever retort from me and then you're going to write that 'Palmer said this, and Weaver said that.' I get it. It's your job. But it's really very simple. I've been together with Earl from 1969 to 1981, and if I can't tell Earl how I feel, if he's so insecure that he can't really hear the truth, that's his problem then."

Boswell didn't get a witty response. No, he got much more. Apparently, Earl hated to be referred to as insecure. If I had known that, I would have described him that way a lot earlier. The next night, Earl and his wife, Marianna, went out to a Baltimore restaurant owned by Hersh Pachino called the Orchard Inn, where Earl downed about 15 gin and tonics. I know the precise number because I was a regular at the restaurant and later heard the whole story from my pals there. At some point during the evening, Earl told one of my friends that I could call him any expletive I wanted but that he wouldn't tolerate being called insecure.

Marianna, who also had a few drinks that night, had the good sense to take a taxi back to their home. Earl, however, insisted on driving and he didn't make it far before he got pulled over for zigzagging all over the road. When a police officer approached his Cadillac, Earl had trouble figuring out how to roll the window down. The officer asked him his name and if he knew where he was. He couldn't answer either question. The officer asked Earl to get out of the car and checked to make sure that his erratic driving wasn't due to poor health. "Do you have a physical infirmity, sir?" he asked.

Suddenly, the guy who didn't know his name or whereabouts sprung to life. "Yes, I do. Jim Palmer."

Earl is sitting on a curb between two parking meters in the process of getting a DUI, and *I'm* his problem.

Earl loved me. Earl hated me. But together we figured out a way to forge an extremely productive relationship and achieve excellence.

VISIT TO THE MOUND

We don't live our lives in a vacuum. No, we are all products of our environment—from birth until adulthood. Report cards provide a window into what society values in its citizens. Although it's important that children learn math, reading, writing, and science, there's a reason that most schools also let parents and guardians know whether their child "plays well with others." Socialization is important. And it goes a long way toward determining our levels of happiness and productivity.

Parental influence plays a significant role in that process. Though I didn't have a conventional upbringing, I ended up with the three key ingredients I needed to go out into the world with confidence: supportive parents, strong friendships, and a passion for athletics. I realize that not everyone grows up in ideal conditions. Parent-child relationships can be difficult. Sometimes enduring friendships don't come until later in life. And it can take time for some of us to find our true passion.

Don't sweat the small stuff. Getting bogged down in petty differences is counterproductive. We all come to the workplace with different backgrounds, ages, and styles, but hopefully with the same goal of achieving personal and organizational success. But that requires employees to "work well with others." Is it possible to alienate your co-workers and still get ahead? Yes, it probably is. But is that the kind of worker and person you really want to be? I doubt it.

It's a delicate balance. While we want to get along well with our colleagues, we don't want to spend too much time socializing on the job. And while some of us click well with our co-workers, we struggle to connect with or find ourselves disagreeing with our bosses. Robert Townsend, the former CEO of Avis Car Rental, really nailed it when he remarked, "A good manager doesn't try to eliminate conflict. He tries to keep it from wasting the energies of his people. If you're the boss and your people fight you openly when they think that you are wrong, that's healthy."

As Tommy Lasorda used to say, "Keep the five guys who know hate you from the 20 guys who haven't made up their minds."

How do you approach your boss when you have a problem? Or do you choose to just hold your tongue rather than raise concerns? An open dialogue is almost always preferable to allowing problems to fester. Now I'm not encouraging you to go out and publicly pick a fight with your boss. Choosing the right place, time, and manner to talk with your boss about issues is imperative. The company picnic and the birthday celebration in the break room probably don't qualify as good times or places. Earl Weaver and I were in a line of work and had the type of relationship that allowed for a public airing of grievances. But I reserved my most important conversations with Earl for behind closed doors.

If you lack ability, you can't perform. But if you can't work well with others, you can't perform optimally.

5TH INNING

Excelling

A FTER YOU'VE SOAKED UP THE KNOWLEDGE, IMPLEMENTED what you've learned, battled through initial hard times, and grasped how to build effective professional relationships, you are in an ideal position to flourish. At that point it's a question of pulling together all the strands of information you've gathered and proceeding with a winning combination of confidence and know-how. I never could have imagined that the first five years of my major league career would be so eventful. From the exhilaration of making a meaningful contribution to a World Series-winning team to staring down the reality that I might never pitch again, I felt battle-tested and ready to continue my baseball journey.

As the 1960s gave way to the 1970s, I had a lot I wanted to accomplish. First and foremost, I wanted to remain healthy so that when my manager handed me the ball every four days I would be ready to help my team. In my three previous injury-plagued seasons, I had pitched a total of 230 big league innings. In 1970 I wanted to prove that I could shoulder a heavy workload without breaking down. It was a great thrill to accomplish that goal. I ended up leading the American League in innings pitched that season with 305, making my first All-Star team, and notching my first 20-win season. That represented the start of an amazing decade for me, as I worked within a well-defined team framework to achieve personal excellence.

I once read a book called *House* that helped me understand why and how the Orioles became such an exemplary organization during my career. The book had nothing to do with sports. Rather, it dealt with the construction of a 3,000-square-foot house in rural Massachusetts. Now that might sound dry and unappealing to the vast majority of us who lack ties to the construction industry or a strong interest in the homebuilding process, but it ended up being a fascinating read with universal application. In describing every step of the building of this particular house from the blueprints to the banging of nails to move-in day, Pulitzer Prize-winning author Tracy Kidder made me better grasp the concept of excellence on a baseball field and beyond. The couple that commissioned the house was akin to the team owner and other front-office people, the architect was the manager, and the construction company was the players.

How did the Orioles, a team born out of failure, build their house? It started with the development of a blueprint for success after the club moved from St. Louis to Baltimore in 1954. For the St. Louis Browns, excellence was always a distant notion. To be fair, the Browns faced obstacles that other teams didn't, starting with the fact that the locals had another better option, the Cardinals, who lived in a shiny mansion on the hill. And the Browns couldn't do much right on the field, finishing no higher than sixth in the American League in their last eight seasons in St. Louis. But at least they had some laughs before closing shop, thanks to Bill Veeck, who bought the team in 1951 and promptly instituted a series of out-of-the-box promotions intended to garner fan interest. One of those stunts involved putting 3'7" Eddie Gaedel in the box against the Detroit Tigers. Not surprisingly, Gaedel walked on four pitches. He never came to the plate again.

In serious financial straits and uncharacteristically out of ideas, Veeck saw no other option but to leave town. He would have relocated to Milwaukee after the '52 season if the Boston Braves didn't beat him to the punch. Baltimore was his second choice, but he didn't win enough support from league owners to make the move. Still in St. Louis in 1953, Veeck had to unload some of the organization's best players just to pay the bills. Only after Baltimore lawyer Clarence Miles took the team off of Veeck's hands did the other owners allow the team to head east to Maryland.

The organization didn't experience immediate prosperity in its new home, but at least fans, many of whom had probably grown weary of the lowly Washington Senators, showed up to support the Orioles. More than a million people passed through the gates in

My sister, Bonnie, my mom, Polly, and I pose for a picture in New York City in 1951. (Courtesy Jim Palmer)

My older sister, Bonnie, and I are together when we lived in New York City circa 1952. (Courtesy Jim Palmer)

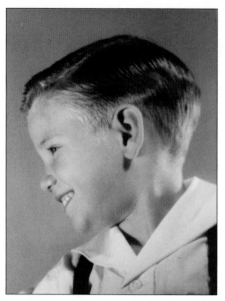

I have fond memories of growing up in New York. (Courtesy Jim Palmer)

I stand next to my parents, Moe and Polly Wiesen, in a very Mad Men*-esque picture. (Courtesy Jim Palmer)*

I was nicknamed "Cakes" because of my traditional pregame meal, though I doubt I finished this stack of pancakes. (Courtesy Jim Palmer)

Here I am pitching for Scottsdale High in Arizona, where I also was all-state in football and basketball. (Courtesy Jim Palmer)

Left: Only 20 years old, I stand next to my idol, Sandy Koufax, prior to Game 2 of the 1966 World Series, where I amazingly outperformed the legendary pitcher. I was shocked at how well we played. (AP Images)

Below: Third baseman Brooks Robinson (No. 5) celebrates our 1966 World Series title with catcher Andy Etchebarren and pitcher Dave McNally after the final out. I felt like I was on top of the world, but tougher times lay ahead.

Pitching coach George Bamberger and I plan strategy for the upcoming season during spring training in Miami. (Courtesy Jim Palmer)

The high leg kick was part of my pitching mechanics, which I refined through extensive work.

I was part of a great staff in 1971. From left to right, Dave McNally, Mike Cuellar, me, and Pat Dobson each won at least 20 games that season.

Above: During my major league career, the mental aspect was just as important as the physical one.

Right: I take great pride in that I spent my whole career with one franchise.

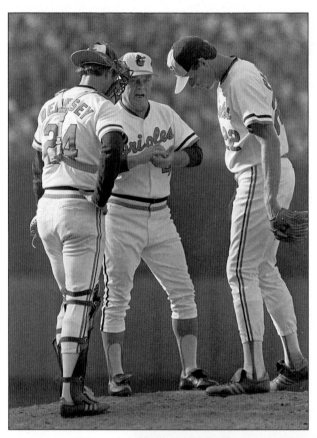

Earl Weaver and I had a complicated and sometimes heated relationship, and catcher Rick Dempsey hated it when we started yelling at each other during visits to the mound. (AP Images)

The Robinsons—Brooks (left) and Frank (right)—were great teammates, and the Hall of Famers were a major reason we went to the World Series multiple times. (USA TODAY Sports Images)

1954 to watch carryovers from the Browns roster lose 100 games. The house had serious structural flaws.

The original architects of "The Oriole Way," a set of core principles that helped guide the Orioles to an enormous period of success from the mid-1960s to the early 1980s, were Paul Richards, who served as manager and general manager of the team from 1955 to 1961, and Jim McLaughlin, the organization's first scouting and minor league director. Richards and McLaughlin weren't revolutionaries, but like many successful businessmen, they applied good, old-fashioned common sense to running a company, starting with placing an emphasis on building from within by creating a first-class farm system. To accomplish that goal, they hired additional scouts to fan out across the country and evaluate young talent.

The other key components of Orioles philosophy were building around pitching and mastering fundamentals. In 1955 *Sports Illustrated*, then just a year into its run, had the foresight to label Richards a "baseball mastermind." Richards himself didn't consider what he was doing a closely held secret. In fact, he wrote a book and a series of columns for *SI* that spelled out his ideas on organizational development and baseball strategy. He understood that while the overarching approach of "The Oriole Way" was important, it was hugely dependent on the front-line people in charge of teaching the methods behind the philosophy. He adapted his book into an instructional manual that he handed to minor league instructors, including Cal Ripken Sr. and Earl Weaver. In 1960 the system started producing results; the franchise's first winning season since 1945 signaled a turning point. No longer an American League doormat, the organization had designs on becoming an overachieving small-market team that could compete with the traditional powers in New York, Detroit, and Cleveland.

I got a crash course in "The Oriole Way" in 1964 at minor league camp in Thomasville, Georgia, and at Single A ball in Aberdeen, South Dakota. Prior to working with Cal, Earl, George Bamberger, and the other instructors, I went out and played baseball without thinking too much about the intricacies of the game. It didn't occur to me that a team that plays fundamentally sound baseball gives itself a significant edge over the course of a long season.

Though they didn't articulate it at the time, probably because the phrase didn't really exist back then, Richards and McLaughlin and their successors sought to create a "corporate culture" that would permeate every corner of the organization, including talent evaluation, coaching, and playing. We hear the terms "corporate culture" and "organizational culture" thrown around all the time these days. But what do they really mean? In their book *Corporate Culture and Performance*, Harvard Business School professors John Kotter and James Heskett get to the heart of the concept's two-tiered meaning: "At the deeper and less visible level, culture refers to values that are shared by the people in a group and that tend to persist over time even when group membership changes…At the more visible level, culture represents the behavior patterns or style of an organization that new employees are automatically encouraged to follow by their fellow employees."

The Oriole system was based on this type of continuity. At each stop on the minor league ladder, instructors taught fundamentals the same way. When you got to the majors, you knew what was expected of you and didn't have to learn the finer points of how to play. To the casual fan, baseball is a game of highlights. Towering home runs, tremendous catches, or close plays at the plate tend to stand out more than when a fielder hits a cut-off man, a base runner goes from first to third on a single, or a hitter makes an out but advances a runner. Ken Singleton, who played 10 seasons with the Orioles from 1975 to 1984, nicely summed up the importance of doing these little things right. Asked by *The Washington Post* to define baseball fundamental, he said, "It's any baseball act that is so simple that the man in the stands thinks, 'I could do that. Why can't those big leaguers?'" Earl Weaver had his own spin on the idea. He referred to baseball as "pitching, three-run homers, and fundamentals."

David Packard, the co-founder of Hewlett-Packard, defined teamwork thusly: "A group of people get together and exist as an institution we call a company so they are able to accomplish something collectively that they could not accomplish separately." That, in a nutshell, was "The Oriole Way."

Even the best systems will fail without the right people operating them and carrying out their ideals. One player who definitely made the Orioles special was the man they called "Mr. Oriole," Brooks Robinson, who played his entire 23-year career in Baltimore.

Brooksie arrived in Baltimore in 1955, a year after the team relocated from St. Louis. It was a lean period for the Orioles and their young third baseman. The team's first winning season in Baltimore in 1960 coincided with Brooksie's breakthrough season. Still just 23 years old, he won his first Gold Glove and finished third in American League MVP balloting. In 1964 he won MVP. By the time I got to the Orioles the following season, he had established himself as a team leader.

Any player who wins a major league record 16 Gold Gloves is going to go down in the annals of baseball history as a defensive marvel. Brooksie had lightning quick reflexes that allowed him to spear grounders or line drives that no mere mortal would have had a shot at. (If you haven't had the privilege of seeing him in action, I suggest going on YouTube to catch some of his unbelievable plays.) Describing a player as "old school" has become trite, but it's what Brooksie was to his core. He went about his business in the most professional way possible, led by example, and treated everyone with respect. He never hot-dogged a play. Current Orioles third baseman Manny Machado is a great fielder, but, like a lot of players over the years, he likes to put a little unnecessary flair into some of the plays he makes. Brooksie never drew attention to himself. He just suited up and played the game—2,896 times, to be exact.

So much has been said and written about Brooksie's defense that his offensive gifts tend to get overlooked. He saved some of his best at-bats for when the team most needed a clutch hit. If we trailed by a run with two outs in the ninth inning, he's the one I wanted to step out of the on-deck circle. We probably wouldn't have won the 1970 World Series without him. He hit an incredible .485 in that postseason. Beneath his folksy homespun façade, he had the heart of a competitor.

Brooksie's play and leadership profoundly impacted the team's fortunes, and the way he conducted himself as a person helped teach his younger teammates how to interact with each other and the public. Everyone who played with Brooks thought the world of him. Rick Dempsey, whose excellence behind the plate contributed enormously to the success I enjoyed in the second half of my career, likes to talk about when he came via trade to Baltimore in June 1976 uncertain about his future in the game and surrounded by strange faces. The first guy to really take the time to talk to him was Brooksie, who was hitting less than .150 at the time. In good times and in horrible times, he treated people kindly. That is an incredible trait. He treated fans with equal courtesy. It's easy for celebrities to act in an aloof manner, to have bloated egos, and to treat fans as an inconvenience or, worse, as the bane of their existence. Through his actions, which consisted of blocking out time before games to chat with fans, Brooksie taught me the importance of making yourself accessible to the people whose support helps pay your salary. It's fitting that the 1971 Norman Rockwell painting of Brooks shows him signing a baseball for a young fan leaning over a railing at the ballpark.

It was the addition of a second Robinson in 1966 that really took our ballclub to the next echelon. Frank Robinson spent six of his 21 Hall of Fame seasons in Baltimore, and it's no coincidence that the Orioles went to the World Series four of those years. Our front office did a stellar job of balancing a largely homegrown pitching staff with a lineup that combined players who came up through our system and players acquired via trade. General manager Harry Dalton was responsible for wresting Frank from the Cincinnati Reds, with whom he had spent 10 very productive seasons. During a racially tense period in this country, Brooks, a white southerner, effusively welcomed Frank to the team, sending a loud and clear message to everyone in town that he was a member of the Orioles family and deserved to be treated with respect.

The big difference between our 94-win team in 1965 and 97-win team in 1966 was that the '66 team featured Frank in the middle of the lineup. Advanced metrics calculating how many additional wins a player accounts for show that to be true. Mostly because he did it in such a way that I knew he would make my job easier, I'll never forget the first time I witnessed Frank hit a baseball in an Orioles uniform. It came during an intra-squad scrimmage at spring training. Frank had arrived a little late because he was up in Baltimore looking for a place to live. But the lack of batting practice didn't affect him in the least. Steve Cosgrove threw him a wicked 12–6 curveball that had started to drop, when Frank got out on his front foot and laced a line drive off the left-field chalk line for extra bases. After seeing that piece of hitting, I turned to my teammate Dick Hall in the dugout and said, "I think we just won the pennant." I was only partly right. We won the *World Series* that season. Frank made everyone in the lineup better. He was a huge presence. And he had an edge to him. He and I didn't have too many extended conversations, but I attribute that to his general dislike for pitchers. Yes, we were teammates, but I was still someone whose job consisted of trying to get the better of hitters like him. After the '68 season, I played on a Puerto Rican League team that Frank managed. He didn't say much that winter either, but if he had, I certainly would have listened.

By the time we landed him, Frank had lost a lot of his speed and defensive range and couldn't get much on his throws due to a bum right shoulder. But he continued to play the game with total professionalism. He gave the team a swagger. And in 1966 he also gave us 49 home runs and 122 RBIs. More importantly, his production prompted the Orioles brass to refine their strategy for building a sustained winner. If you take a team with strong pitching and top-notch defense and add to it a guy or two who can hit three-run home runs, you're going to win a lot of games. The Earl Weaver era was proof of that.

Frank played the game by the book. And he would be very hard on himself when he experienced a rare mental lapse. During a game at Fenway Park in the early 1970s, Frank hit a towering fly ball to left field that he thought would clear the Green Monster. He went into his home run trot early—only to see the ball carom off the wall and into the glove of Carl Yastrzemski, who threw a dart to second base to hold him to a single out. After the game a contrite Frank strolled into Earl's office and dropped a couple of $100 bills on his desk with a note that read, "I embarrassed the team and I embarrassed myself. It'll never happen again." And I'm pretty sure it never did.

Brooks and Frank were the marquee names of that era, but without the contributions of some lesser-known teammates, we might not have reached the same levels of excellence. In *Good to Great*, another book I'd recommend, author Jim Collins discusses the approaches that organizations can take to achieve top-level results over an extended period of time. As Collins writes, "Leaders of companies that go from good to great start not with 'where' but with 'who.' They start by getting the right people on the bus, the wrong people off the bus, and the right people in the right seats."

It's interesting that Collins refers to the "right people" rather than the "best people." In some cases the right people happen also to be the best people, but that's not always so. In a team setting, it's more important to create an environment where all the passengers on the bus know their roles and embrace the goals of the organization. If you have passengers who are loaded with talent but can't work well with others and complain all the time, you're probably better off getting them off the bus.

Without the contributions of many, our accomplishments would have been far fewer. A couple of guys really personified "The Oriole Way" during those golden years. One of them was my good friend Davey Leonhard. Few guys had better minor league careers than Davey, who went 66–21 between 1963 and 1967. Despite those impressive numbers, Davey never griped when he got to the majors and found himself mostly relegated to bullpen duty. A Baltimore-area native, he wanted to play for the Orioles even if that meant being the last man on the staff. He stayed in shape, showed up prepared, and committed himself to helping the team in any way he could. All of that work resulted in just 16 career wins, but the chance to pitch in two World Series made it all worthwhile for him.

Mark Belanger is another Oriole I think of when the conversation turns to those special years. Mark played with the Orioles from 1965 to 1981, meaning his major league career almost completely overlapped with mine. Mark wasn't much with the bat, hitting just .228 for his career, but defensively, he set a new standard for excellence. *The Hardball Times*, a statistics-laden baseball publication, calculated that Mark saved more than 35 runs with his glove in 1975, the best defensive season for a shortstop in major league history. Astoundingly, Mark hit a home run in his first ever postseason game in 1969 and then played 42 more playoff games without going deep again. But it didn't matter what he did at the plate. Only Mark Belanger could have hit .225 and .226 in two consecutive seasons and still earned votes for American League MVP. In true Orioles fashion, he took younger infielders under his wings and taught them how to play defense as a unit.

Belanger set a standard for greatness at shortstop. Paul Blair did the same in center field. He prevented a lot of bloopers from falling in for hits by playing very shallow. But because of his speed and instincts, rarely did he get burned by a ball hit over his head. Our corner outfielders had the luxury of playing the lines because Paul could cover so much ground in the outfield.

Our offense during those years got a major boost from some guys not named Robinson. Don Buford, a second baseman who Earl moved to left field, developed into one of the best leadoff hitters in the game from 1969 to 1971, scoring 99 runs in each of those seasons. Boog Powell is another guy whose contributions helped make us perennial contenders. Always a steady hitter, he took his offensive game to an even higher level in '69, when he finished second in MVP balloting, and '70, when he won the award with a monster 35 home-run, 114-RBI season. Boog became a household name through his many appearances in Miller Lite commercials, but he was more than just a big personality. He was a great hitter, too.

I'm glad we found room on the bus for Terry Crowley in the early 1970s. Crow put up prodigious numbers at Triple A Rochester in 1969 but found himself in a battle to make the big league club in 1970. In one of our last spring training games in West Palm Beach, he got the start at first base against the Atlanta Braves. It was a final

Few organizations ever achieve excellence, let alone sustain it.

I became an Orioles fan in 1956 after the team relocated to my hometown of Scottsdale, Arizona, for spring training. Later, I basked in their 20-year run of excellence from 1964 to 1983, a period made even more special by the contributions of my good friend and former high school classmate, Jim Palmer.

Firmly believing in the parallels of excellence between team sports and business, I mused about what could be learned from the O's extraordinary period of excellence. My family's 120-year-old newspaper and public service organization, *The Seattle Times*, is a case study in commitment to excellence. Each of our six generations has been committed to responsible stewardship, the belief that it is a privilege to lead the enterprise, and to the notion of serving the community and leaving the enterprise in as good as or better shape for the next generation.

Fiercely independent journalism and robust public service are our core values and purpose. These tenets drive our culture and help us attract great team members. They are what empower our *Times* family to continually strive for the excellence that is essential to surviving and thriving in an ever-changing and hyper-competitive environment.

In 1985 we established a goal of becoming one of the nation's best regional newspapers. In the 30 years since, we have been awarded seven Pulitzer Prizes and are in the top five nationally for Pulitzer finalist nominations. On the business side, we became the second largest printed newspaper on the West Coast in 2015 with the most visited news website in the Pacific Northwest. We are creating new forms of journalism in areas like public education. We are on the cutting edge of transforming to a digital-first future. And we remain one of the country's last locally owned independent metro newspapers.

At the end of the day, our success is like the 1964–83 Orioles. Both of us had a shared purpose and vision, a commitment to organizational and individual excellence, uncompromising expectations, and a short set of inviolate values.

—FRANK BLETHEN, PUBLISHER OF *THE SEATTLE TIMES*

chance for Crow to show Earl that he deserved to start the season in Baltimore. We took a one-run lead into the bottom of the ninth inning, but the Braves got their leadoff hitter on and tried to advance him to second with a bunt. Crow came in to field the ball but couldn't get it out of his glove fast enough to get the lead runner. A single tied the game, and the Braves went on to win. Crow was devastated, realizing that his lack of fundamentals helped cost us the game. He knew that players who committed this type of miscue would incur the wrath of Earl. And sure enough, as we left the field, Earl went up to Crow and yelled, "If you want to make this club, you have to make that play!"

Today, Crow would have texted or called his wife's cell to let her know to make plans to travel to Rochester for the start of the Triple A season. But back in less technological times, he could do nothing but sit and stew on the bus ride from West Palm to Miami. When the bus pulled into Miami, Earl greeted Crowley at the bottom of the stairs. "You made the fucking club," he growled. "I'll talk to you tomorrow." The next day Crow reported to the field extra early feeling good at having made the team. When Earl spotted him, he ordered him over for a chat. "This is the way it's gonna be," Earl hissed. "If you're lucky, you might play once a week. But you have a good chance of pinch-hitting two or three times a week. So get your ass ready, so when I use you, you'll be productive. Welcome to the club. If you can't do the job, I'll get someone else." Earl punctuated his remarks with a poke to Crow's chest.

With Earl, you always knew your job description. There was no gray area. He told you your role and his expectations of you and let you take care of the rest. He had high standards, but no one could ever plead ignorance to that fact. Earl trusted everyone on the club to do his job, and we felt like we owed it to him to live up to that trust.

Just as Earl promised, he didn't put Crow in the starting lineup very often in 1970. But he gave him ample opportunity to come off the bench in critical situations. Crow responded with three game-winning home runs that season. After winning back-to-back World

Series with the Reds and then moving on to the Braves, he returned to the Orioles from 1976 to 1982, finishing his career with 108 pinch-hits—tied for 13th most in baseball history.

Ask this trivia question the next time you're in a group of baseball fans: who led the Orioles in batting average in both 1970 and 1971? Anyone who answers correctly on the first try is either an expert on Orioles history or a big Merv Rettemund fan. Merv, like Crow, settled into a comfortable role as a bench player and spot starter for us, hitting .322 and .318 in the seasons that we went to back-to-back World Series. Those were career years for Merv, who ended up a hitting .271 in his 13 major league seasons.

When an organization figures out the right way to do business, it sets itself up for long-term prosperity. The Orioles teams of the late '60s and early '70s had strong management and leadership and a group of players who understood that winning is a process that starts in spring training and ideally ends with a World Series parade. There was nothing fluky about it. The Orioles executed a carefully thought-out plan for success.

A year after coming up short against the New York Mets, we won 108 games during the regular season and returned to the World Series to face the Reds. For the first time in my career, I started Game 1 of a Fall Classic, a somewhat odd decision on Earl's part, considering I was a high fastball pitcher, and the first seven guys in Cincinnati's lineup, including Pete Rose, Tony Perez, and Johnny Bench, were all high fastball hitters. Mike Cuellar or Dave McNally, both of whom had nasty curveballs, would have been more logical choices, but Earl decided to take his chances with me. After Lee May took me deep in the first and third innings to give the Reds a 3–0 lead, it looked like Earl had blundered. But I managed to settle down and keep Cincinnati at bay the rest of the night. Meanwhile, Brooks and Boog homered, and we rallied for a 4–3 win at Riverfront Stadium. Another come-from-behind win the next night put the Reds in a deep hole that they couldn't dig out of. We beat the Reds in five games to secure the second World Series title in franchise history. A lot of people remember that series as the one where Brooksie made a number of incredible defensive plays at third base to go along with his .485 average in the playoffs.

In 1971 the Orioles' long-held belief in the value of strong starting pitching paid off royally when McNally, Cuellar, Pat Dobson, and I all reached the 20-win mark, making us the last starting rotation to boast four 20-game winners in a season. A lot of people don't realize that we did it in 158 games due to a number of rainouts that weren't rescheduled. I don't see any staff accomplishing that feat again. With the apparent permanence of five-man rotations and pitch counts, it's increasingly rare to have four 20-game winners in an entire league, let alone on one team. I was the last of the group to notch his 20th win, doing so in my final start against the Cleveland Indians. As a team we "only" won 101 games in '71, compared to 109 in '69 and 108 in '70. We eclipsed the 100-win mark for the third year in a row despite not having an everyday player who hit .300 or 30 home runs. Unfortunately, after sweeping the Oakland A's in the American League Championship Series, we came up short in the World Series, losing in seven games to the Pittsburgh Pirates.

If it weren't for the A's, there's no telling how many World Series we may have won or at least participated in during the 1970s. The A's put a damper on our 1974 season by again beating us in the ALCS, but the late-season surge that got us to the postseason remains among my most cherished memories because it demonstrated how dedicated to excellence we were as a ballclub. On August 29, we sat in fourth place in the division, eight games out of first place. A doubleheader sweep of first-place Boston in early September that featured a pair of 1–0 victories brought us within three games of the division lead. On an off day before the final game of that series, we convened a players-only meeting at Paul Blair's house to talk about what we needed to do the rest of the way to catch Boston. Our strengths were apparent: pitching and defense. But the razor-thin margins of our doubleheader wins against the Red Sox demonstrated a weakness for scoring runs. Nobody on the club hit 20 home runs that season, so waiting for a three-run home run to bail us out of games didn't seem like a viable option. We needed to get inventive. As a team we decided to bunt and hit and run more. Now, that might sound like a mutiny, but as proponents and practitioners of "The Oriole Way," we understood the value of assessing a situation and figuring out what adjustments needed to take place.

We followed up the back-to-back 1–0 wins against Boston with three more shutouts to pull even closer to the top spot. And we implemented our strategy of advancing runners with bunts and being aggressive on the base paths. Earl wondered why we were bunting and running without signs, but he couldn't (and didn't) argue with the results. We finished the season on a 28–6 run to win the division.

I'm not recommending that you flout your boss' authority by disobeying orders or implementing your own plans without consent. Following protocol is important. If Earl had put his foot down and demanded we stop putting on our own signs, we would have obeyed. But there was a trust between us that allowed for creativity.

Earl and I sparred constantly over who knew more about our team. For a couple of years, I had urged him to never to rest Blair when I was pitching. In 1975 I felt I had lost a couple of games because Earl had insisted on playing 35-year-old Jim Northrup in center field instead of Blair. Ideally, I wanted Earl to go a step further by giving me a chance just once to fill out the entire lineup card. With 12 games left in the '76 season, we were 10½ games out of first place, so Earl felt it was as a good a time as any to get me off his back by letting me serve as player-manager in the first game of a doubleheader at Yankee Stadium. When I arrived in the clubhouse that morning, Earl put three pieces of paper in front of me. He had written a different lineup on each.

"Pick one," he instructed.

Pick one? This wasn't the deal.

"Earl, I thought you were going to let me make out my own lineup," I said.

"Nope, not gonna happen," Earl replied, shaking his head. "If you did that and we won, then everybody would know you were smarter than I am."

I looked down at the first lineup and noticed that Blair wasn't in it. I crumbled it up and threw it in the garbage can. I moved on to lineup No. 2. I didn't see Blair's name in that one either. Again, I wadded up the piece of paper and chucked it into the can. The whole point of this exercise was to make sure I had our best defensive players behind me. Two of the three lineups guaranteed that wouldn't be the case. I prayed that Blair's name appeared on the last piece of paper. And much to my relief, it was there. I pitched a four-hit shutout that day. We won 2–0. Blair made nine putouts in center field. I think I proved my point, and so did Earl. He was never going to turn over the reins of the team to a know-nothing pitcher like me.

The best tribute to the Orioles' on-field leadership in the 1970s was how many coaches eventually assumed leadership positions with other teams. George Bamberger, our pitching coach, became skipper of the Milwaukee Brewers and New York Mets. Jimmy Frey, our first-base coach, went on to manage the Kansas City Royals and had stints as manager and general manager of the Chicago Cubs. Bill Hunter, who coached third base, got a managerial job in Texas. And Cal Ripken Sr. got a shot at managing the Orioles in the 1980s.

VISIT TO THE MOUND

From the time we enter school and start getting graded for our work, we understand the various words used to evaluate us. We all yearn for the parental approval (and accompanying monetary reward) that often comes with getting an "A" and we shrink in fear at the thought of getting a test or report card with the letter "F" on it. It's interesting that every letter grade except for "F" has an adjective attached to it: excellent (A), good (B), average (C), passing (D). The F grade, on the other hand, has a dreaded noun accompanying it: failure. It is an ugly word, and from a young age, we know it's to be avoided at all costs. The other letter grades describe you. The F grade defines you.

Everyone strives for excellence. When we're young and still figuring out our core values and beliefs and exploring our abilities, our primary motivating factor for bringing home a good report card is to please others. It's normal to want the validation of parents, teachers, and other authority figures. As we get older, however, and develop a better sense of ourselves, the motivation to be our best emanates more from within. As adults we still hope that others approve of what we do. That's human nature. But we're also aware of the risks of doing what others want at the expense of doing what we think is best for us. In the workplace we seek praise from superiors either verbally or in written evaluations.

What are your goals? It's a favorite question of job interviewers that cuts to the heart of your future in the workplace. Whether or not you're on the interview circuit, take some time and answer the question with a focus on what you want to achieve in five, 10, 15 years, not where you want to be. Figure out what you want to do before you set your sights on where you want to be. Accomplishments lead to promotions.

Ideally, what others expect of us will coincide with what we expect of ourselves. A championship team is a great lens through which to view that concept. A team with World Series aspirations should share the common goal of achieving excellence, and there should be an unspoken understanding that each member of the team will do what he can to make himself and his team as good as it possibly can be. The preceding chapter chronicles a team that achieved true excellence. It wasn't the last team I played on that reached that level, but it stands out for me because it was the first. What makes a team or any unit truly excellent? I'd argue that exemplary organizations almost always feature the following: team members who understand and embrace their roles, a culture where the whole of the unit becomes greater than the sum of its individual parts, and an environment where team members feed off each other's successes.

Ask yourself how close your organization is to achieving excellence. Are individual roles well-defined? Does everyone contribute to the larger team framework? Is there healthy competition between employees, and do they work to make each other better? If you're leading an organization, are you creating this kind of culture for them? Do you know what your employees' goals are and do you have a plan for helping them meet their objectives?

I'm not downplaying the importance of individual accomplishment. There's nothing wrong with striving to earn a promotion or a pay raise. Generally, hard work that benefits an individual also helps the larger organization. It's not an either/or choice between personal and team success. There might be times when you put your own needs over the needs of the team. And there might be times when you, as they say in sports, "take one for the team."

6TH INNING

Sustaining Success

I T TAKES A LOT OF HARD WORK, PLANNING, AND ACU-
men to build a strong company or team to go from good to great.
The Orioles had the necessary people and plans to accomplish that
goal in the 1960s, but an equally important part of the story is the
steps the organization took to sustain that level of success over the
next decade and a half, an eternity by baseball standards.

It is interesting to see how great organizations evolve when
market conditions change. Remember when there was a Blockbuster
video store on every corner? Then Netflix came along and changed
how we watch movies. The same goes for Amazon, which helped
put Borders out of business 20 years after Borders did the same
to several small bookstore chains. The Internet has transformed
us in a lot of ways, including as consumers. It has made dozens of
other industries obsolete and has fundamentally changed the way
we consume information, putting encyclopedias and many print
newspapers on the endangered species list. The bottom line is that
industries evolve. Baseball is no exception.

Major League Baseball's fundamental shift in how it did business
took place in December 1975 when an independent arbitrator named
Peter Seitz ushered in the free agency era by ruling that teams didn't
have the right to treat players as lifetime property. That ruling didn't
just come out of nowhere. For several years Marvin Miller and the players association had fought tooth and nail against the "reserve clause,"
which restricted players from leaving their current teams to seek more
lucrative deals elsewhere. Outfielder Curt Flood's refusal to accept a
trade from the St. Louis Cardinals to the Philadelphia Phillies after the
1969 season culminated three years later in a U.S. Supreme Court ruling that upheld the reserve clause, but the attention that Flood brought
to the issue paved the way for Seitz's pro-labor ruling three years later.

My former teammate Dave McNally, along with fellow pitcher Andy Messersmith, became the new faces of the challenge to a practice that Flood and some of his supporters compared to slavery. After winning 181 games with the Orioles, Dave finished out his career in Montreal, playing his only season there without a contract. Even though he had decided to retire from the game, Dave was an ideal candidate in Miller's eyes to declare for free agency. Dave, who served as our union rep in Baltimore, agreed to get involved in the fight. To try and thwart his participation, the Expos offered him a two-year contract worth a lot more than the $115,000 he had made the previous season. But Dave didn't take the bait.

The Seitz ruling had a major impact on the make-up of our 1976 team. With Reggie Jackson and Ken Holtzman both in line to declare for free agency after the '76 season, the Oakland A's felt it made sense to try and get something in return for them before they signed elsewhere. So a week before Opening Day, we sent Don Baylor and Mike Torrez to the A's in exchange for Reggie and Holtzman. On paper it looked like we got the better of the deal. Torrez was coming off a 20-win season, but he didn't have Holtzman's track record of winning 18 or 19 games nearly every season. And Baylor could hit, as later evidenced by his 1979 American League MVP award, but he was no Reggie, who had already blossomed into one of the all-time great home run hitters. The trade for Reggie rivaled Frank Robinson's 1965 arrival in Baltimore in terms of its potential to vault the Orioles into World Series contention. We won it all in Frank's first season with the team, and it was realistic to think that Reggie could help deliver a title in '76.

I had a long history with Reggie. Back in the summer of 1965, I saw him play in an amateur baseball league in Baltimore, where his mother had moved when Reggie was a kid. He attended Arizona State University at the time, and it only took a few at-bats to realize he possessed major league talent. In the early 1970s, Reggie and the A's were our perennial nemesis, beating us in the American League Championship Series in 1973 and 1974. Overall, I handled Reggie as well as could be expected, the two long balls he hit off me in the 1971 American League Championship Series notwithstanding.

Considering his enormous talent, it would have been nice if Reggie had played the whole season for us. But he felt his services were worth more than the $140,000 or so that the Orioles were obligated to pay him under the terms of his expiring contract with the A's. He knew he was going to cash in once he became a free agent after the season, but he didn't want to wait until then. To force the issue, he announced that he simply wouldn't play until the Orioles met his demands for a pay increase. Nearly a month of the season passed before general manager Hank Peters blinked and agreed to pay Reggie $200,000 for the '76 season. That meant, as Dave Anderson of *The New York Times* pointed out, that Reggie earned a 43 percent raise for missing 20 percent of the season. This didn't sit well with the team's other unsigned players, including Holtzman, Bobby Grich, and Mike Flanagan, who weren't given similar in-season raises. The acrimonious start between Reggie and the team also didn't bode well for his long-term future with us. And his holdout also irritated a lot of Orioles fans. But here's the thing about Reggie: he made it known from the moment he put on an Orioles uniform that he really didn't care what people thought about him. And that included Earl Weaver.

I genuinely liked Reggie. He was the nicest guy in the world... except for the times that he wasn't. It all depended on his mood that day. Sometimes he'd exude warmth and graciousness. Other times, he would be incredibly standoffish. The two of us had great rapport based on mutual respect, even when we weren't teammates. He used to call me "Diamond Jim," which I always took as a compliment until he revealed to me years later that there was a wholesale men's clothing store by that name in his native Philadelphia.

For many people 1976 is remembered for the festivities surrounding America's Bicentennial, but in American League cities across the country that year, Reggie Jackson and George Washington got nearly equal billing. Reggie's post-1976 plans became a recurring subplot everywhere we went with writers querying Reggie on their city's chances of landing him. When a writer in Milwaukee asked him if he would consider signing with the Brewers, Reggie ruminated for a few seconds before delivering the good news that he liked beer and bratwurst and the bad news that he didn't think Milwaukee was the right place for him. In response to the same question from an Indians beat writer, Reggie said he would keep an open mind about Cleveland because it had a federal reserve bank.

Reggie played the game hard and he played it with flair. And his flamboyance made him a target. In the second game of an August doubleheader against the Chicago White Sox, Reggie smacked a

I learned early on that baseball is a hard game. It is tough to do well every game, and I found that out when I made my major league debut in September 1955. After going 2-for-4 in my first game, I ran back to the hotel to call my mom and dad. I remember telling them, "This is my cup of tea!" I was surprised at how easy it was. Well, needless to say, I went hitless in my next 18 at-bats and struck out 10 times. Baseball is a hard game. Even harder is sustaining success.

It seemed that people were always amazed at how even-keeled I was as a baseball player. I knew that we had 162 games to play. Whether I played well or didn't play well, I knew that I would be coming back to do my job the next day. It is a long season, and if I went 4-for-4 or 0-for-4, I approached the game the same way.

Hoot Evers was my first roommate in the majors. I was 18 years old, and Hoot was 34 years old. He gave me a lot of good advice, but the best advice he gave was to play the game hard and not to celebrate if you get four hits or beat yourself up if you go hitless. It is a long season. I would watch teammates and opponents break bats or bust up coolers when they didn't do well. That never made sense to me because it didn't change the result.

A lot of our success depends on other people. You can go 4-for-4, and your team can still lose the game or you can go hitless, and your team can win. I played in four World Series. The two we were supposed to win, we lost (1969 and 1971). The two we were supposed to lose, we won (1966 and 1970). You can never predict outcomes in baseball and in life, and that is why you always have to do your best and prepare for the long haul.

—BROOKS ROBINSON, HALL OF FAME THIRD BASEMAN

fifth-inning grand slam off of Ken Brett, George's older brother. As Reggie rounded second base, he kind of stopped in place and started jawing at Brett and the White Sox infielders. Apparently, Brett's pitches during his previous at-bat were a little too inside for Reggie's liking. Reggie couldn't be blamed for being a bit oversensitive. A few weeks earlier, he had left a game on a stretcher after Dock Ellis of the New York Yankees hit him in the face with a pitch, a situation I'll talk more about in the next chapter because it was the only time in my career that *I* threw at a hitter.

When Reggie came up in the seventh inning, everyone sensed that trouble might be on the horizon. And sure enough, reliever Clay Carroll's first pitch came right at Reggie's head. Fortunately, he ducked out of the way, hitting the ground with a thud. As the tension in the air thickened, Reggie sat on top of home plate at Memorial Stadium for a few seconds, thinking about his next move. Then he slowly took off his glasses, which everyone in an Orioles uniform took as a cue to start spilling out onto the field. The White Sox, who had some really big guys like Lamar Johnson and Pete Vuckovich, quickly joined us once Reggie hurled his bat at Carroll and charged the mound. This was the season that White Sox owner Bill Veeck dressed his team in short pants. So there we were fighting an army of big uglies clad in shorts. There were skirmishes all over the place. Johnson wore a catcher's mask during the brawl. And Tony Muser, our backup first baseman, got sucker punched by his good friend, White Sox pitcher Bart Johnson. After what seemed like 20 minutes, things finally settled down. But when we went back onto the field in the eighth inning, Muser, still upset that his friend had slugged him, almost charged the White Sox dugout.

After we swept the doubleheader, Reggie returned to the hotel that he was calling home, which happened to be the White Sox team hotel. In the lobby he ran into White Sox broadcaster Harry Caray, who had yet to move to the north side to become the voice of the Cubs. Harry didn't like what he saw from Reggie that night and made sure Reggie knew it. According to the *Chicago Tribune*, Harry got in Reggie's face and told him he didn't appreciate the "bush exhibition" he put on. Reggie angrily told Harry that he wouldn't allow pitchers to jeopardize his career by throwing at him. He even invited Harry up to his hotel room to see pictures of what his face looked like after getting beaned by Ellis earlier that season. Harry declined the invitation.

White Sox manager Paul Richards, one of the original architects of "The Oriole Way" in the '50s and '60s, admitted after the game that Carroll had knocked Reggie down in response to his "hot-dog act" on the base paths. I have a lot of memories of that game, none more vivid than how awful Richards looked in those shorts.

Reggie put up decent numbers in '76. If he hadn't missed all of April, he would have almost certainly finished with 30-plus home runs and 100-plus RBIs. Who knows what kind of season we would have had if Reggie had been in the lineup from day one? As it stood, we struggled out of the gates, and despite going 48–32 after the All-Star break, we couldn't catch the New York Yankees, who lost in the World Series to the Big Red Machine.

Off the field, Reggie had a good head on his shoulders that enabled him to maximize his earning potential. For at least a little while, it looked like he had genuine interest in continuing his career in Baltimore. Hank Peters reportedly offered him a five-year, $2.5 million contract, but George Steinbrenner outbid us, prompting Reggie to choose to wear Yankee pinstripes for the next five years. Holtzman was already in the Bronx when Reggie arrived. After two and half solid months with us, we traded him to New York, along with Elrod Hendricks, Doyle Alexander, Jimmy Freeman, and Grant Jackson, in return for Rick Dempsey, Tippy Martinez, Rudy May, Scott McGregor, and Dave Pagan.

In November of 1976 on the occasion of receiving my third Cy Young award, I turned a routine photo op with a few canned quotes into an off-the-cuff commentary on what I viewed as the potential complications of free agency. "When I came into baseball, it was astute men with astute organizations who ran the winning teams," I said. "Now if you need a player and don't have one in your system, you take out your checkbook. This is going to fatten the bank accounts of a few selfish players, but it may hurt baseball. What about the balance of the league, and the cities like Baltimore that can't afford it? The Yankees, I think, bought the pennant with a checkbook this year."

Looking back, that opinion might seem a little harsh, but you have to understand my thinking at the time. Of course, I had Reggie very much in mind when I made the comments. I felt that by virtue of his holdout, he had cost us a chance at winning the division. But the issue transcended Reggie. I had spent my entire career in an organization that put a high premium on unity, cohesion, and consistency. The Orioles transformed themselves into a competitive club based on these concepts. As I think I've made clear, I'm a firm believer in workers getting adequately compensated for the services they provide. For years, I had put winning games ahead of making money, but that didn't mean I thought owners had license to grossly underpay players. Still, I worried that unfettered free agency would damage the integrity of the game. And in some ways, it has. Players have become much more transient, not staying in one place very long. Prior to free agency, successful organizations were built through the draft and trades. Starting in the mid-1970s, it became much more about money. Do you remain loyal to a longtime employer who you feel should be compensating you more generously? Or do you jump ship and switch employers in order to cash a fatter paycheck? It's a question many of us face at some point.

Not long after criticizing the notion of "checkbook baseball," I realized that the times were changing and that I needed to stand up for myself. It didn't hurt my bargaining position that I had won my third Cy Young award in '76. I knew the kind of money Reggie and Grich were offered to stay in Baltimore, so I hired a lawyer to help me renegotiate my contract. I made about $180,000 in '76 and felt I deserved closer to $300,000 for the coming seasons, the same amount Grich was seeking. At first, Peters didn't budge, but I took a page from Reggie's playbook the following spring training and threatened to sit out until the team negotiated with me. Finally, they offered me $275,000 a year with a possible bonus of $15,000 if I made a "significant contribution" to the club that consisted of winning at least 20 games, earning the Cy Young award, and posting a sub-2.50 ERA. Not one of those things. *All* of those things. In 1977 I won 20 games, finished second in Cy Young voting, and had a 2.91 ERA.

The early years of free agency were rife with cautionary tales. Take my teammate Wayne Garland, who went down in baseball history as the first major free-agent bust. In 1976, his first year pitching primarily as a starter, Wayne won 20 games for us. After the season he signed a 10-year deal with the Cleveland Indians worth $200,000 a season, not including possible bonuses. He went 13–19 in his first season in Cleveland and was never the same pitcher again after undergoing rotator cuff surgery the following year. A couple of months before he hung up his spikes in 1981, Wayne spoke candidly about how he was an early beneficiary of the free-agent sweepstakes. "Nobody knew the fair price for a 20-game winner, but they shelled out all that money," he told *The New York Times*. "I wasn't worth it, but nobody was worth it. I didn't ask for it, but I'd have been a fool not to take it."

People are free to form their own opinions about Marvin Miller's legacy and about unions in general. My feelings about Marvin were probably best expressed by the vote I cast in 2010 to induct him into the Hall of Fame. He fell one vote shy of enshrinement that year and remains on the outside looking in. He passed away in 2012. To some owners the idea of Marvin in Cooperstown is anathema. But the truth is that the owners are the ones who created him by opposing any form of free agency or arbitration for years and years. Nobody did more to change the landscape of baseball than Marvin.

The drama surrounding Reggie dominated the headlines in '76, but in retrospect that blockbuster deal with the Yankees turned out to be equally significant to the Orioles in the long run because Tippy, Scotty, and Demper became key contributors to our next wave of success in the late '70s and early '80s. Ron Guidry almost came our way in that trade, too, but we'll just put that one in the what-might-have-been category. Rudy May, another player we got in the deal with the Yankees, pitched very well for us before we traded him to the Expos after the '77 season for outfielder Gary Roenicke and pitcher Don "Stan the Man Unusual" Stanhouse. The right-handed hitting Roenicke and the left-handed hitting John Lowenstein, whom we picked up off of waivers from the Texas Rangers, formed a very successful platoon in left field from 1979 to 1982. And Stanhouse saved a total of 45 games for us in '78 and '79. In the age of free agency, Peters showed that general managers could still build teams through smart trades.

As it turned out, 1978 was my last great year. For the fourth consecutive season, I won at least 20 games. It was the eighth and final time that I would reach that mark. I led the American League in innings pitched four times, and that didn't even include the 1975 season, in which I threw the most innings of my career (323). With the 1970s drawing to a close, I confronted the reality that I was slowing down. I still had enough left in the tank to hold down a spot in a talented rotation, but as tends to happen when you get older, my body couldn't withstand the rigors of pitching 300 innings a year.

My evolution from pitching ace to pitching aide was gradual, but the process really started to accelerate in 1979. After starting the season 6–2, I came down with arm soreness that took me out of action for much of June, July, and August. During that time I had ample opportunity to observe our young starting pitchers, a group including Flanagan, McGregor, and Dennis Martinez that was drawing the inevitable comparisons to our outstanding staffs of the early 1970s.

Flanny emerged as an ace that season, winning a league-leading 23 games and the Cy Young award. He had a tremendous ability to change speeds, using his off-speed pitches to set up his sinker, which was one of the best in the majors. I told you earlier in the book about the crisis in confidence that he experienced in his first full season in the big leagues and how Earl's words of encouragement back then helped turn him into the pitcher we all knew he could be. Mike and I grew very close. I considered him a friend and confidante. After his playing career ended, he remained a vital part of the organization—first as pitching coach and later as vice president of baseball operations. He eventually left the front office and joined me and Rick Dempsey as Orioles broadcasters. Flanny was like a brother to me, so it was heartbreaking when he took his own life in 2011. I just didn't know the inner turmoil he must have felt. I don't think anyone did. I choose to remember Flanny at his best, so 1979 remains a special season in my memory. Behind our customary strong pitching and an offense carried by Eddie Murray and Ken Singleton, we won 102 games and reached the World Series. After taking three of the first four games against Willie Stargell and the Pittsburgh Pirates, it looked like we would bookend the decade with titles. But then Pittsburgh won three games in a row, the last two in Baltimore, to prevent that from happening. I had a chance to pitch us to victory in Game 6, but after throwing six shutout innings, I yielded a pair of runs in the seventh and eighth innings and took the loss. There's nothing quite like celebrating a championship with your teammates and fans, and 1979 will always feel like the one that got away. On the positive side, our success that season proved that, even in the free agency era, "The Oriole Way" still worked. Flanny joked that we had a pitching staff full of Cys—he was Cy Young, I was Cy Old, Steve Stone was Cy Present (after winning 25 games in 1980), and Storm Davis was Cy Future.

Flanny, McGregor, and I formed an inseparable trio. Scotty, a Southern California kid drafted out of high school, spent the first four seasons of his career in the Yankees' minor league system. At 19 years of age, he reported to his first spring training and found himself in the presence of legends like Mickey Mantle and Whitey Ford, who came by to give pointers to the young players. When he found out he got traded to the Orioles, Scotty cried. The guys in the Yankees system had become like family, and he felt like he would be starting over in Baltimore. But he quickly figured out that his new band of brothers was going to integrate him into our system and look out for him in every way. Regardless of who was on the mound, we all pitched every game together. For 162 games we sat and studied every pitch of every contest.

I encouraged Scotty to work at keeping hitters guessing by changing speeds, a formula that I saw Mike Cuellar and Dave McNally perfect earlier in my career. On the final day of the 1980 season, Scotty and Len Barker of the Indians faced off in a match-up of two guys going for their 20th win of the year. Scotty pitched lights out to reach that individual milestone and to give us 100 wins as a team.

I could no longer contribute as much to the team's success with my arm, so I resolved to help my younger peers with my words. As I've said, the Orioles' status as a model franchise had a lot to do with continuity from one generation to the next, so my willingness to work with my teammates was more of an unwritten mandate than a choice.

That's not to say that my advice was always heeded. Before a series in Kansas City, I gave reliever Sammy Stewart some tips on how to handle George Brett. "Okay, Sam, here's the deal," I explained. "Brett is a good enough hitter that he can pretty much hit a single to left at will against a right-hander. So you either give him a single or you let your ego take over and come inside on him, and he'll take you to the waterfall at Royals Stadium."

A couple of nights later, Sammy came in to pitch the 16th inning of a 4–4 game. Brett was the first hitter he faced. He threw a fastball on the inner-half of the plate, and Brett deposited it in the waterfall for a game-ending home run.

I tried to lead by example, and by winning 16 games in 1980, I think I demonstrated that I still deserved a spot in the rotation. But it was getting harder to put my pitches exactly where I wanted them. I tried to compensate for the deterioration of my skillset by living up to my reputation as a "thinking man's pitcher." If I couldn't routinely throw shutouts any more, I would try to prevent my opponents from scoring runs in bunches. That was my mind-set even in my prime, and it probably helps explain why I never yielded a grand slam in my career.

In the strike year of 1981 I had the first losing season of my career. In September, some Orioles fans turned on me. After I surrendered four home runs in two and two-thirds innings against the

A's, I heard a chorus of boos from the Memorial Stadium faithful. That hurt. I won't lie.

I got off to a miserable start in 1982, which didn't thrill Earl, who announced at the start of the season that it would be his last as manager. In early May I had an ERA of 6.84. Ten years earlier Earl would have brushed off my early struggles as an aberration. But coming on the heels of three injury-plagued seasons in a row, I think a lot of people, including Peters, questioned whether I had a future with the team. Earl had similar concerns and he bought himself a little time to think about the situation by temporarily giving my spot in the rotation to Stewart. I didn't take the news well. I knew that my slow start was attributable to neck spasms, and a move to the bullpen made zero sense to me. For the first time in my career, I entertained the idea of asking for a trade. But then I thought better of it. If Hank and Earl felt I needed to prove myself to them, I vowed I would do just that. I would show them that I wasn't washed up.

I harkened back to the lessons I learned in the late 1960s, when I nearly saw my career end prematurely due to arm problems. Over the course of the next two weeks, I pitched in relief four times. In between appearances I ran, I threw, I prepared, and I didn't pout. I wasn't happy about the demotion, but I figured the only way I could regain my status in the starting rotation was to show I could still pitch. The act of entering a game already in progress felt unfamiliar, and other than a perfect four-inning stint against the Seattle Mariners, my performances in relief didn't do much to convince Hank or Earl that I could contribute to the team's success. A poor relief outing on May 18 led to a loss to the Minnesota Twins that dropped us eight games out of first place. Only a little more than a month into the season, we were already flirting with irrelevance.

At the age of 36, I was in jeopardy of losing my seat on the bus. My body no longer had the ability to withstand the aches and pains it had earlier in my career. No longer at the top of my game, I continued to share my wisdom and know-how with the younger members of the pitching staff. Robin Roberts had mentored me in 1965, and now it was my turn to carry on the tradition.

My teammate Storm Davis, who was a 20-year-old rookie for us in 1982, reminded me of myself at that age. Like me, he had quickly risen through the ranks of the Orioles minor league system and arrived in Baltimore with high expectations. He had all the tools. With the right work ethic and a little bit of refinement, I felt he could become a mainstay of the pitching staff. Storm knew all about me from his father, an Orioles fan in Florida, who tried to get his son to emulate my pitching motion. Storm looked up to his dad, so in turn, he grew up admiring me. The media seized on our similarities and anointed him the next Jim Palmer. That put a lot of pressure on him and made it all the more important for me to show my support and give him guidance. Out in the bullpen, I talked to him about the importance of keeping his body in shape and locating his pitches. We developed a kinship. Some of our teammates jokingly called us "Ward and the Beav," referring to the wholesome father and son on the old TV show *Leave It to Beaver*. When Storm wanted to know something that I couldn't teach him, I found someone who could. During a game in Detroit, I asked Tigers pitching coach Roger Craig to show Storm how to throw a split-fingered fastball, a pitch he soon added to his repertoire.

I have to think that the time I spent working with Storm helped put me back in touch with myself. After rejoining the starting rotation at the end of May, I didn't lose a game between Memorial Day and Labor Day and finished the season with a 15–5 record. In an article headlined "The Fall and Rise of Jim Palmer," Tom Boswell of *The Washington Post* wrote, "Certainly, what no one in baseball expected in 1982 was that Palmer would win 11 consecutive games and do it so masterfully that a rational claim can be made that at this moment he's once again the best starting pitcher in the American League." Boswell was surprised at my resurgence, and so was I.

We fell nine-and-a-half games out of first place in May but battled back to make it a race in September. With five games left in the season, we trailed the first-place Milwaukee Brewers by a seemingly insurmountable four games. Unfortunately, the '82 campaign ended on a down note for me and the team. Entering the final weekend of the season, we still trailed the Brewers by three games, but we still controlled our own fate because we had a four-game home series against Milwaukee that included a Friday doubleheader. We swept the twin bill and then won again on Saturday, setting the stage for a decisive 162nd game of the season. As if that wasn't enough drama, the game featured several other compelling storylines. It would be Earl's last game (for the time being) in an Orioles uniform. The game also boasted a pitching match-up of two of the most success-ful pitchers of the 1970s—myself and Don Sutton. Together, we had combined for more than 500 wins in our careers. Coming as it did during an NFL players' strike, the nationally televised Sunday afternoon game promised to draw a lot of eyeballs.

I just didn't have good stuff that day. I gave up four solo home runs, including two to Robin Yount, who won the American League MVP that season. When Earl came out to get me in the top of the sixth inning, we trailed 4–1. Before I handed him the ball for the last time, he reminded me of how much success we'd enjoyed over the years. I told him I wished I had fared better in our last game together, which we ended up losing 10–2.

Rather than participating in the American League Championship Series, Earl and I were scheduled to meet up in Anaheim two days later to be part of ABC's broadcast of the Brewers-Angels series. Before leaving the clubhouse, Earl gave a reporter for *The New York Times* a last Palmer quote to chew on: "Jimmy thinks he's through with me, but he's not. I'm depending on him. He's got a little experi-ence in that booth. But he's carried me for 15 years. He can carry me another week. I was just hoping he could carry us for two or three innings today, but it didn't work out that way."

The loss to Milwaukee was one of the most bitter of my career. I felt I cost the team a spot in the postseason and Earl a chance to go out on top. Not everyone realized how personally I took that game. Bob Maisel, a writer for *The Baltimore Sun*, wrote a preposterous column asserting that I didn't care if we won or lost because I had the postseason job with ABC lined up. It's one thing when people who don't know you make assumptions about your character and actions. That can be brushed off as idle chatter with no basis in reality. But Maisel had hung around Memorial Stadium for decades and he should have known better than to question my motivation level. The column bothered me. Fortunately, I had grown a pretty thick skin after playing the game for so long, so I didn't let it get to me. My daughter, Kelly, who was 13 years old at the time, was a different story. She got so upset at Maisel that she picked up a pen and wrote him a letter...which *The Sun* published under the headline, "A letter from a Palmer fan."

"Every time that I have seen an article that has said something bad about my dad, I have wanted to write a response letter," Kelly wrote. "So I finally decided to write one on the last game of the season that my dad pitched. I wish once, when my dad lost, that someone would compliment him on how well he tried and that he had done the best he could. His arm had been hurting before Sunday's game, and we both had decided that if he won, he won, and if he lost, he lost, but he would try his best to win, like he always did."

I didn't know Kelly wrote the letter until one of the production guys at ABC told me about it while we were out in Milwaukee. Needless to say, it meant the world to me that my daughter would defend my honor so eloquently and so publicly.

After Game 3 in Milwaukee, an ABC producer named Dennis Lewin asked me if I wanted to grab some dinner. Sure, I said. He wanted to know if it was okay if Earl joined us. I said of course it's okay if Earl wanted to come along. Dennis went off to invite Earl, who apparently didn't believe I was telling the truth. "Does Jim really want me to go?" he asked Dennis. Earl realized that our player-manager relationship had ended and that I was no longer obligated to spend time with him. But you know what? I had spent the better part of 14 seasons with the guy. A two-hour meal wasn't going to kill me. The situation said a lot about Earl. When he took off the Orioles uniform for the last time, Earl was no longer the little general. In less than a week, he had become a different person.

It felt strange not to see Earl around at spring training in 1983. But we were in good hands. Joe Altobelli, who had managed 11 seasons in Baltimore's minor league system before joining the Yankees coaching staff for a couple of seasons, knew our way of doing things as well as anybody.

Joe realized that it was always about getting the right 25 people on a bus that started its trek in spring training with the goal of driving all the way through to the World Series. In August 1983, in the thick of a pennant race, we were trying to separate ourselves from a crowded field of five American League East teams that all had a legitimate shot at winning the division. We were trying to go from good to great and entering play on August 24 we were half a game behind the first-place Brewers.

Some games help define a season, and the "Lenn Sakata Game" in 1983 definitely qualifies as one. On that night we rallied for two runs in the bottom of the ninth inning against the Toronto Blue Jays to send the game into extra innings. But then we ran into a problem. In an effort to tie or win the game in the ninth, Altobelli had Lenny, a middle infielder, pinch hit for backup catcher Joe Nolan, who, earlier in the game, had pinch hit for starting catcher Rick Dempsey. That left us with no catchers left to use.

Not many people remember that Lenny was the Orioles' starting shortstop when a blossoming star named Cal Ripken Jr. came onto the scene in 1981. Before joining the Orioles, Lenny had spent a number of years in the Brewers system. He was a fundamentally sound player who could capably play shortstop or second base. In his seven years in the big leagues, he had never put on the catcher's gear in a game situation. But with our club in desperate straits entering the 10th inning, Lenny volunteered to strap on the catcher's gear and move from second base to behind the plate. Altobelli had to further improvise by putting Gary Roenicke at second base and John Lowenstein at third, positions that neither usually played. Lenny didn't make the offer to catch on a whim. He had experimented at the position during spring training scrimmages and caught bullpen sessions, all in the event that a situation like this one might someday arise. Even he couldn't have imagined that it would happen in the middle of a pennant race.

It was an unusual sight watching massive reliever Tim Stoddard throwing warm-up pitches to Lenny, a Hawaiian-born, Japanese American who was generously listed at 5'9". The odd-couple battery didn't produce good results. Toronto's Cliff Johnson led off the inning with a go-ahead home run, and after Stoddard yielded a single to Barry Bonnell, Altobelli replaced him with Tippy Martinez. And that's when things got really interesting. The Blue Jays couldn't wait to run on Lenny. Bonnell showed his intention by taking a sizeable lead off first base, anxiously waiting for Tippy to release the ball to home plate. The anticipation overwhelmed him because he broke too soon, and Tippy threw to first baseman Eddie Murray, who zipped the ball over to second base to throw out Bonnell. Tippy then walked the speedy Dave Collins, who a few seasons earlier had stolen 79 bases. Collins' body language showed he had every intention of running on Lenny. But he wandered too far off first base, and Tippy picked him off. Willie Upshaw followed with a single, and in a shocking repeat of what had just happened, he, too, got picked off.

Leading off the bottom of the 10th, Cal re-tied the game with a home run. Later in the inning, with two on and two out, Lenny came to the plate with a chance to play hero. And he did just that, blasting a game-winning homer off of Randy Moffitt. That game proved that Lenny Sakata was one of the right 25 guys to have on the bus in 1983. I love that story. That's why I closed my Hall of Fame speech with it.

Then there's Cal. It's easy to look at someone like Ripken Jr. and just assume that he always had it easy. He literally grew up an Oriole, soaking in all the knowledge his father and the other coaches in the organization had to offer. At 13 years of age, he stood six feet tall and already looked like a big league ballplayer. If ever someone was born to wear black and orange, it was him. And he got that opportunity when the Orioles selected him out of high school in the second round of the 1978 draft. In the last two of his four seasons in the minors, Cal showed that he could handle Double A and Triple A pitching. But the test of whether he could make it at the highest level started with his promotion to the Orioles a few weeks after the 1981 strike ended. Cal, who turned 21 shortly after his call-up, got just five hits in 39 at-bats that season, not a great start to a career but not a reason to write a guy off either. The trade of Doug DeCinces to the California Angels after the '81 season opened up an opportunity for Cal to play third base every day. On Opening Day of 1982, he got three hits, including his first career home run, in a win against the Kansas City Royals. Then he went into the kind of hitting slump that can doom the career of a young player, going 4-for-55 through May 1. Imagine the pressure he was under. As the son of an Orioles coaching legend, he had something extra to prove to anyone who thought his daddy pulled strings for him. A lot of people in his position would have thought to themselves, *Maybe I don't belong here.* During those tough early days, I remember him sitting in the corner of the clubhouse and crying. Fortunately, Cal had the mental fortitude to work through his early struggles. He had a solid May, an incredible June, and in July took over for Belanger as the club's starting shortstop. He finished the season with 28 home runs and 93 RBIs and received the American League Rookie of the Year award.

We would not have been able to sustain our success into the 1980s without a terrific combination of youngsters like Cal and Murray and veterans like Dempsey, who became a backbone of the team after coming on board in that 10-player trade with the Yankees in 1976. It's funny to think that a guy who became so instrumental to our success felt so forlorn about joining our club in the first place. During his three seasons in New York, Demper had fallen into a comfortable role as Thurman Munson's backup. The Yankees had held down first place in the American League East since early in the '76 season and showed no signs of slowing down. More than anything, Demper wanted to play in the postseason, so the trade to Baltimore disappointed him. On the other hand, he looked forward to the chance of playing regularly with us.

He joined us in the middle of a 10-game road trip. Earl called Demper into his office and told him that he liked how starting catcher Dave Duncan was playing and to be patient until he found a time to insert him into the lineup. Demper didn't see any action for the entire road swing. After the final game of the trip, we returned to Baltimore in the middle of the night. Most of us went home, but the team bus dropped Demper and the other new Orioles off at a Best Western Hotel off Interstate 695. He lugged his three suitcases across the parking lot and went to get his room key. Then he dragged his luggage back across the lot, up a flight of stairs, and down an outdoor hallway. He fumbled for his room key and stuck it in the door. It didn't work. At the end of his rope, Demper picked up his bags and hurled them over a railing to the parking lot below. Each bag opened on impact, scattering clothes all over the blacktop. Then Demper walked back to the stairwell, perched himself on the top step, and had himself a good cry. At that moment he thought his career was over. The clothes got picked up and returned to the suitcases. And during the next homestand, Earl finally gave him some starts. He immediately impressed me and everyone else with his ability to call a game and keep base runners from stealing. On days I pitched, I'd look at Earl's lineup and, if I didn't see Demper in there, I would make sure Earl fixed the problem.

Demper was one of the most hard-nosed players I played with. He would do anything to help his team win, even if it meant risking his physical well-being. In one of the worst home-plate collisions ever, 235-pound Bo Jackson became a human missile and bowled Demper over in 1987, breaking his thumb. But Demper, who was playing for the Indians at the time, held onto the ball and recorded the out.

Demper noticed things on the field that no one else could, including the tendencies of base runners. For example, he realized that runners on third base instinctively take an extra step toward home plate when a pitch is thrown inside to a right-handed hitter. He shared this knowledge with all the pitchers and our third baseman, DeCinces. So whenever that situation arose, I'd come inside and let Demper and DeCinces take care of the rest. I think we picked off Dwight Evans of the Boston Red Sox at least three times using that play. Demper worked out similar arrangements with Eddie Murray at first base. We had enough talent during those years to win a lot of games, but you make the task facing your opponent that much more difficult when you lure them into giving you outs. It was the ability to do the little things that helped distinguish the Orioles from other teams during our long run of success. And I have no doubt that companies everywhere benefit from having employees who pay attention to detail, especially in today's world, where speed is valued over accuracy, and cutting corners has become the norm rather than the exception.

Earl let it be known loud and clear that he would have preferred a catcher with more pop in his bat. During an incredible 24-year major league career, Demper barely reached the 1,000-hit mark and only had 96 home runs. Earl wouldn't hesitate to pinch hit for him if he felt he had a better option on the bench. After all, that's how the Lenn Sakata Game happened. Demper was sensitive about his lack of offensive prowess. He didn't like being a .239 hitter. He felt it defined him in Earl's eyes. I had a different opinion. "Demper," I told him, "you're a terrific catcher. You block the plate. You throw runners out. You'll run through a wall to help us win. You don't need to hit .280."

We tend to measure the worth of a position player by his numbers and the accolades he receives. How many times did he hit .300? How many All-Star teams did he make? How many Gold Gloves did he win? For Demper the answers to all of the above questions were zero. Yet without him, our ballclub wouldn't have been nearly as accomplished.

The 1983 Orioles didn't have as much raw talent as some of the teams I played on in the '60s and '70s, but we managed to get the right 25 guys on the bus. Murray had a great year. And Cal, in his second full season, showed he was a superstar in the making, leading the American League in hits on his way to winning the first of his two MVP awards. McGregor, a finesse pitcher whose 85 mile-per-hour fastball looked like it was coming in at 110 when followed by the steady diet of change-ups and hooks that he threw, paced our staff with 18 wins for his sixth double-digit win season in a row, a streak he'd go on to extend to nine. And rookie Mike Boddicker won 16 games.

Our longtime second baseman, Rich Dauer, had a subpar offensive year but committed only seven errors all season. Meanwhile, I won only five games in an injury-plagued season that included a stint at Double A Hagerstown.

We won our division by six games and took out the White Sox in the American League Championship Series, earning a trip to the World Series. On paper I would have fit in better on the roster of our opponent, the Phillies, the so-called "Wheeze Kids," whose starting lineup featured eight players 30 years of age or older and an aging ace in 38-year-old Steve Carlton. I didn't pitch in the ALCS and had my doubts whether Altobelli would call on me against the Phillies. But with the Phillies leading 2–0 in the fifth inning of Game 3, Joe summoned me in from the bullpen. I pitched two scoreless innings, and by the time I departed, we had rallied to take the lead. I got the victory that night on my 37th birthday, making me the only pitcher in baseball history to win a World Series game in three different decades.

We won three of the first four games against the Phillies, and unlike in 1979 when we squandered a 3–1 series lead, we got the job done, winning in five games. McGregor threw a shutout in the series clincher. Demper got much deserved recognition as series MVP after going 5-for-13 in the series with a home run. Not bad for a .239 hitter. He's the only player ever to win a World Series MVP despite being lifted twice for a pinch-hitter.

My victory in the '83 World Series turned out to be the final highlight of my career, and that was fitting in a way. My two-decade career in Baltimore spanned two generations, and I would have been very disappointed not to have had the opportunity to celebrate a championship with "second generation" teammates like Murray, Singleton, Dempsey, Flanagan, McGregor, and Dauer.

On May 12, 1984, I played my final game in a major league uniform, pitching the final two innings of a 12–2 loss to the A's. Like all of my other appearances that season, it wasn't pretty. In two innings of work, I surrendered four runs on five hits, elevating my ERA for the season to 9.17. Peters made it known that I wouldn't be starting any more games for the Orioles in 1984, and he and Altobelli felt it would be degrading to stick me in the bullpen. So Hank gave me two options: retire or go on the disabled list. I asked for my release because in my heart I felt I could still pitch at the major league level. At the press conference announcing the end of my 19-year tenure with the Orioles, Peters said it pained him to let me go. When I took the podium, I could barely keep my composure. "I really don't know," I said. "I still think I can pitch. I still have the desire to do that. But I'm going to leave. Thank you very much for coming." With that I called an end to the event and drove home.

The California Angels showed some interest in me. Reggie, Grich, and DeCinces, all former teammates of mine, were there, and I liked the idea of playing in the warmth of Southern California. I wouldn't even have been the oldest pitcher on the Angels staff. That distinction belonged to 41-year-old Tommy John, who was still five years away from retirement. When Angels manager John McNamara told me he couldn't guarantee that I would crack the starting rotation, I started thinking seriously about hanging it up. I might have auditioned for a few other teams if I didn't have some other avenues I wanted to pursue.

It's hard to say good-bye to a career you love. And though I found real fulfillment in post-playing-career ventures as a broadcaster and corporate spokesman, I wondered for years after my last major league appearance whether I still had what it took to compete at that level. In 1991, at the age of 45, I decided to scratch that itch. My comeback attempt garnered a lot of attention. It was unusual for a player who had already been enshrined in the Hall of Fame to try such a thing. But it wasn't a gimmick. I had kept myself in shape and genuinely felt like I might be able to help the Orioles, who were managed at the time by my former teammate Frank Robinson. As it turned out, my body couldn't withstand the rigors of trying to throw a baseball past the likes of Frank Thomas and Ken Griffey Jr. While warming up for what would end up being my only appearance of the exhibition season, I tore my hamstring. I then went out and gave up two runs and five hits in two innings to the Red Sox. My fastest pitch was clocked at 75 miles per hour. I might have stuck it out for a while longer if it weren't for my hamstring, but as it stood, it was time to call it a career once and for all.

VISIT TO THE MOUND

You've paid your dues, won the respect of your peers and superiors, and can take pride in looking over your growing list of accomplishments. After you've gotten to that point, the challenge becomes staying there. Probably the biggest enemy of sustained workplace success is burnout, a phenomenon so prevalent that the Mayo Clinic addresses it in an adult health seminar called "Job burnout: How to spot it and take action," defining job burnout as "a special type of job stress—a state of physical, emotional, or mental exhaustion combined with doubts about your competence and the value of your work." In other words, burnout happens when you lose your passion for what you do best. That can be a helpless feeling. Yesterday, you loved going to work, but today you don't. You glide for a while on your natural ability, hoping that you're just experiencing a temporary malaise. But it doesn't go away. So you take a few vacation days, thinking some time off might recharge your batteries. But that doesn't work either. The reality is there's been a fundamental shift in the relationship between you and your work. This happens to a lot of baseball players at the minor league level who realize the game they've been playing since they were just out of diapers is no longer fun or fulfilling. But burnout can hit someone in the middle of their career, too. It's just another form of workplace adversity.

The Mayo Clinic has the following advice for anyone who feels they've become less effective and engaged with their work: identify and manage the stressors that have contributed to those feelings; evaluate your options; adjust your attitude; seek support;

assess your interests, skills, and passions; get some exercise; and get some sleep.

Nobody loves their job all the time. If you do something long enough, you're bound to feel uninspired from time to time. Don't be concerned if you experience symptoms of burnout. There are deadlines, demands, commutes, personality conflicts, and difficulties in balancing work and personal life. I can relate to all of those things. Sometimes I didn't feel like boarding that red-eye flight to California, battling it out with Earl Weaver in the newspapers, or being away from my family for two weeks at a time. The lack of quality time with my daughters was particularly difficult. Sometimes I used to wake them up late at night after returning home from a road trip, realizing that that might be the only hour we would spent together for another few days.

Seize on the opportunity to assess what you and your organization can do to keep you at the top of your game. To sustain a level of excellence, you need to keep perspective. Ultimately, you might decide that you truly have lost your zest for what you do. If that's the case, you can consider switching careers. But in most cases, it's about fending off burnout and rediscovering what you love about what you do and continuing on with a renewed commitment to excellence.

7TH INNING

Diversifying

NO PROFESSIONAL ATHLETE WANTS TO FACE THE REALITY that his or her career has an expiration date. That's why a lot of us keep trying to compete long after Father Time has sent a clear message to hang it up. I can relate to that type of stubbornness. I found it difficult to say good-bye to something that brought me so much satisfaction, and that's why I attempted a short-lived comeback at the age of 45.

I made a good living during my playing career but not enough to retire without worrying about my family's long-term financial stability. That was the primary reason that I chose to make a midlife career change. The other reason was that I genuinely enjoy working and challenging myself. I've seen a lot of retired players with all the time and money in the world to do all the things anyone could ever dream of doing. And some of them couldn't be more miserable. I love golf, but I just couldn't imagine hitting the links every day for the next 50 years of my life. I love spending time with my family, but they understood that I'm a much happier person when I stay busy. In the second act of my life, I decided that I wanted to broaden my horizons, try out new vocations, and become more than just a baseball player. That's what led me to the broadcast booth and work as a corporate spokesman.

In today's professional world, people have to reinvent themselves all the time. Though no official statistics exist to back up the claim, many experts say that the average American worker will go through seven different careers in a lifetime. That may very well be an overestimate, but the point remains that many people change careers either out of necessity or by choice. In my case it was a little of both.

Long before I ever contemplated retirement, I attempted to plant the seeds for a career in broadcasting by doing what amounted to an internship with ABC. My affiliation with the network dated back to 1978 when I had the opportunity to work the American League Championship Series. Truth be told, I wasn't ABC's first choice. That distinction went to Reggie Jackson, who, if available, was slated to join Howard Cosell and Keith Jackson in the booth. As many longtime baseball fans remember, the New York Yankees and Boston Red Sox ended the '78 campaign with identical 99–63 records, forcing the teams to play a one-game playoff at Fenway to determine who would go to the ALCS to face the Kansas City Royals. If Reggie's Yankees advanced, I had instructions to fly to Kansas City the next morning to call that night's game. I packed a suitcase and put it on my bed just in case. For a while it looked like I'd be staying in Baltimore. The Red Sox led 2–0 behind Mike Torrez, who had yielded just two hits in six innings. Then, in the top of the seventh, Bucky Dent launched a three-run homer over the Green Monster to give the Yankees a lead they didn't relinquish. Red Sox fans might hate Bucky for crushing their hopes, but every time I see him, I tell him he was responsible for my big break in broadcasting.

One of the most difficult parts of transitioning to a new career is that you're surrounded by people who have a lot more experience than you. I decided to focus the first part of this chapter on my work with broadcast legend Howard Cosell, not only because the Howard stories are entertaining, but also because I think everyone trying to learn a new trade can relate to my dealings with someone who has an oversized opinion of himself and his contributions to the industry.

As Bucky launched his iconic homer over the Green Monster, Howard was calling a *Monday Night Football* game at RFK Stadium, a real thriller with the final score of Redskins 9, Cowboys 5. At our first production meeting the next morning in Kansas City, he sidled up and asked me if I was nervous about my broadcasting debut. "Well, Howard," I confessed, "I have to say I'm a little apprehensive. I've never done this before."

"Just remember one thing, young man," Howard told me. "Anybody who's ever worked with me has become a star."

Within seconds of meeting the man, he had told me everything I possibly needed to know about him. Howard immediately set out to show me the way. ABC hadn't had time to outfit me with one of those patented gold blazers, so Howard gave me an extra one of his. Howard wore a 43 long, and I was a size 44 long, but the jacket fit just fine. Now that I looked the part, I just needed to figure out how to avoid making a fool of myself on national television.

It can be frightening to try something new, professionally. After so many years in the game, I knew exactly what I was doing on a baseball field. From preparing for starts, to competing in games, to taking care of my body between outings, it all became second nature. All the practice, game experience, and tutelage from some of baseball's finest minds had made me an authority on pitching. The world's greatest surgeons perform incredible work on an operating table, but that doesn't mean they have the ability to articulately explain what they do to the general public. The same goes for ex-jocks who enter the media world. As the first former athlete to make it big in broadcasting, the late Frank Gifford helped blaze the way for guys like me. It's a tribute to Frank's work in the media that he became better known to some for his Emmy-award-winning work on *Monday Night Football* and other ABC programs than for his Hall of Fame playing career. I later learned that Frank struggled mightily to get through rehearsals. But when the red light of the camera went on, he delivered a nearly flawless performance almost every time. Yes, I was told I had a telegenic presence. And I'm sure that ABC liked the fact that I was already known to a wide segment of the population as the guy who posed in his underwear in magazine ads. But looking good is only part of the battle. There's also that pesky part about trying to sound intelligent.

Dating back to adolescence and young adulthood, I never felt comfortable as a public speaker. When I returned home to Scottsdale, Arizona, after my first year with the Orioles, I received an invitation to speak at the local chamber of commerce. I asked what they wanted me to talk about. Your rookie season, the answer came. I barely got through that speech. In the years that followed, I realized that by virtue of what I did for a living people were interested in what I had to say. That gave me incentive to develop the ability to actually express something worth saying. I had no problem giving quotes to newspaper reporters or recording an interview or commercial, but the idea of being on live TV without a safety net still gave me great pause.

In preparing for my on-air debut, I pictured myself sitting in the corner of the dugout during an Orioles game and talking baseball and game situations with Dave McNally, Mike Cuellar, Chico Salmon, Merv Rettemund, and Terry Crowley. Why did the pitcher throw a slider when it was clear that the batter couldn't catch up with his fastball? Would this be a good situation for a hit-and-run? I may not have known the intricacies of broadcasting, but I knew the finer points of baseball. It became a question of taking that knowledge and refining it into a new skill, turning those dugout conversations into on-air banter, albeit in much less profane form.

For a newbie like me, the booth assignment in '78 was ideal. Howard and Keith were old pros, so I focused on following their lead and being economical with my words. That presented an interesting challenge. The more words that come out of your mouth, the better the chance you have of uttering something intelligent… or something nonsensical. There's an art to saying less. It involves picking your spots and making sure the few words you do say carry the most weight possible.

The Yankees rolled past the Royals in Game 1 of the ALCS. I let Howard and Keith do most of the talking as I tried to familiarize myself with the various processes that comprise a telecast, ranging from the mundane part of watching a game from the press box for the first time to the challenging task of following cues from producers. Unlike when I was holding court in the dugout, I had to be mindful that people at home wanted to know the details of what was going on in the game. That required learning not to talk over pitches.

I rode out to the ballpark for Game 2 with Howard, who was engrossed in the game story in that morning's edition of *The Kansas City Star*. Its headline was something to the effect of, "Drats! Foiled Again By Those Damn Yankees!" To Kansas City sportswriters and fans, it looked like '78 would be a repeat of '76 and '77 when the Yankees beat the Royals to advance to the World Series. In the car Howard wondered aloud which Royals player he should request for a pregame interview. The team's star hitters, George Brett or Amos Otis, seemed like obvious candidates, but I had another thought. And since Howard asked my opinion (sort of), I felt comfortable chiming in. "Why don't you talk to Freddie Patek?" I said, referring to the Royals' speedy and diminutive shortstop.

Howard looked at me like I was crazy. "Young man, listen to me," Howard replied with a look that nearly froze my soul. "Why would I want to do that?"

I didn't back down. I told Howard that Patek knew the pain of defeat better than anybody. The previous October he had grounded into a game-ending double play in deciding Game 5 of the ALCS and then had watched forlornly from the home dugout as the Yankees celebrated another pennant. "He's a 5'5" overachiever. He plays with heart," I said. "If you talk to anybody else, you're just going to get the same old story line about making key pitches and getting key hits. You want to talk to somebody who will tell it like it is."

That last line resonated with Howard, who believed he was put on this earth to give people straight talk. He booked the interview with Patek, who gave Howard and the viewing public an earful about what he expected from the home fans in Game 2. "There are only about 30 people in this city who think we can win," Freddie proclaimed. "Our fans need to get off their rears and start clapping like Yankees fans because we have a chance to win this."

That afternoon the Royals jumped out to an early lead and broke the game open in the seventh inning on the only postseason home run of Patek's career. As little Freddie rounded the bases to thunderous cheers from the stands, Howard uttered a line so perfect that it almost made me forgive him for acting like such a buffoon most of the time. "Just like in the classic Broadway show *Damn Yankees*, you got...to...have...heart!"

I helped create that storyline by insisting that Howard interview Patek, but Howard seized upon it like no one else could. That night, Howard made me come up to his room to watch Game 1 of the National League Championship Series between the Los Angeles Dodgers and Philadelphia Phillies. He gave me pointers while critiquing the broadcast.

Working that series made for a memorable debut. Game 4 of the ALCS took place on a college football Saturday. Keith, who was in Dallas broadcasting the Red River Rivalry game between Texas and Oklahoma that afternoon, boarded a Lear jet and made it to Yankee Stadium 20 minutes before we were scheduled to go on air. Bob Uecker was all mic'd up and ready to go in case Keith didn't make it. Bob and I slapped Keith on the back and congratulated him on his tight balancing act. From the corner of the booth came a loud "harumph!"

"Now you know what kind of schedule I'm always on," Howard informed everyone.

It was always about Howard. That didn't make him a bad guy. It just made him Howard Cosell.

The Yankees won Game 4 to send the Royals home for a third straight year.

In some ways Howard Cosell became my new Earl Weaver. I had an antagonistic relationship with both, but at the end of the day, I knew we shared a common goal. Earl and I wanted to win as many ballgames as possible, and Howard and I wanted to announce ballgames in a way that enhanced the viewer experience. I respected a lot of what Howard did. No one knew the value of a strong storyline better than he did. And no one could touch his ability to turn a phrase. When it came to the intricacies of the game, however, I felt he should have deferred to me. That didn't happen, though, because Howard proudly deferred to no member of the jock-ocracy. That was okay with me. As I grew more comfortable in the broadcast booth, I didn't hesitate to respectfully disagree with Howard if he pontificated too much or expressed a wild opinion about what he thought a manager should do. This created angst for Howard, who took his complaints about me to Roone Arledge, the most powerful man at ABC who oversaw both the network's sports and news divisions.

I'm not sure what I did exactly to raise Howard's ire during Game 3 of the 1981 World Series. I confess I was paying more attention to whether Fernando Valenzuela of the Dodgers might supplant me as the youngest pitcher ever to pitch a World Series shutout, a record I held onto when the Yankees scored four runs off Fernando. The next day I arrived at Dodger Stadium in somewhat of a surly mood. The hot water at the Beverly Wilshire Hotel had gone out overnight, and my hair was not cooperating. The first person I ran into was Dennis Lewin, a producer who would later go on to become a senior vice president at ABC Sports. "Roone called and he said to lay off Howard," Dennis informed me.

"Lay off Howard?" I repeated. "What does that mean?"

"You keep correcting him."

"Well, maybe he shouldn't talk so much."

Whatever transgression I may have committed in Dennis' eyes didn't keep ABC from continuing to seek my services. My first regular season foray into broadcasting came after the Orioles released me in May 1984, and I signed a four-year deal with ABC. Two weeks later I was in the booth with Don Drysdale doing a Cincinnati Reds-Dodgers game for ABC. At the time I felt like I still had enough left in my arm to help a team make a pennant push, but I also realized the chance to do steady work at the network level was too good to pass up. My exact duties that season would be determined by Howard's schedule. If he wasn't available to do a game, I'd work alongside Howard's usual partners, Earl Weaver and Al Michaels. Otherwise, I'd be paired with Don on the backup game of the week.

That July ABC dispatched us all to San Francisco for the All-Star Game. A four-man booth, especially one that included Howard and Earl, would have been untenable, so I was tasked with delivering in-game reports every couple of innings. Back then the game was a much bigger event than it is today even without the Home Run Derby and the pretense that the game actually counts. In the mid-1980s, close to 30 million people tuned in to watch the Midsummer Classic—triple the viewership it garners today. ABC prided itself on its in-depth coverage of the event, which included sending our entire crew out to Candlestick Park to do advance work for the following night's telecast. The assignment didn't please Howard, who would have much preferred pontificating at the hotel bar with a cold beverage. From the time we left the hotel, Howard made it clear to everyone in the car that he had no interest in this part of the job. He wanted to broadcast the game—not run around gathering pregame quotes from players. But we all knew the real reason Howard wanted to avoid windy Candlestick: he was worried about how his toupee would hold up in the blustery elements. Sure enough, the winds were whipping off the San Francisco Bay that afternoon, wreaking havoc with Howard's hairpiece, which went permanently off-center as it struggled to cling to his head. Candlestick Park was on the verge of following through on the threat that Muhammad Ali levied against Howard during one of those old Dean Martin roasts. The toupee barely survived the afternoon. And on the ride back to the hotel, Howard took out his anger on Candlestick Park, wondering why a stadium had been built so close to the bay. "What do you expect, Howard?" Al asked. "Candlestick is a monument to political chicanery."

Howard seemed appeased by Al's answer, which included a short sermon on the questionable land deal that led to Candlestick coming into existence. As Howard mulled it over, Al leaned over and whispered in my ear, "I guarantee you that Howard will work that line into the broadcast tomorrow night."

The next night we all took our positions in the booth as the ABC graphics flashed across the screen. Howard, as was customary, prepared to introduce the game and the broadcast team.

"Hi, everybody, this is Howard Cosell. Welcome to the 55th All-Star Game, coming to you from Candlestick Park, a monument to political chicanery." A broad smile broke out on Al's face. Just 15 seconds into the broadcast, Howard had delivered.

The ultimate Howard Cosell incident took place during Game 2 of the 1984 American League Championship Series between the Detroit Tigers and Royals. "Stay tuned for *Nightline* with my good friend, Teddy Koppel, immediately following our broadcast except on the West Coast," Howard reminded viewers, stretching every syllable of the sentence to its absolute breaking point. During the course of the night, he had delivered four or five *Nightline* promos, each a little more effusive than the previous. And on the final one, which took place as the game went into the 10th inning of a 3–3 game, he decided to just keep going. "My good friend, Teddy Koppel, is there anyone better?" he asked.

We didn't know exactly what was in the cup that Howard was drinking from, but we were starting to get a pretty good idea. Al and I remained silent on the Teddy Koppel question, but then Howard turned and addressed Al directly. "Alfalfa, what do you think of our good friend, Teddy Koppel?"

"Howard, I echo your sentiments," Al responded curtly, hoping to put an end to the ridiculousness and shift the focus back on the baseball game.

Howard didn't approve of the answer, however. "You know the problem with you, Alfalfa, you never ever take a stance on anything!"

During the next commercial break, Howard got up in Al's face and issued him a stern warning: "Fuck with me, little man, and I'll bury your ass!"

I couldn't believe what I was witnessing. *Jeez*, I thought, *Aren't we supposed to be a team up here?*

When we came back from break for the top of the 11th inning, I hoped Howard had gotten the bile out of his system figuratively, at least, though there was precedent for Howard emptying the contents of his stomach during a game. It happened during a November 1970 *Monday Night Football* broadcast with Don Meredith's cowboy boots getting the brunt of the damage.

I was pleased when the first two Tigers batters reached base off of Royals reliever Dan Quisenberry, a development that pretty much forced Howard to pay heed to what was happening in the game. The next batter up tried to sacrifice the runners to second and third, but he bunted the ball too hard, allowing the Royals to throw out the lead runner at third. That gave me a perfect opportunity to chime in with some meaningful analysis. I explained that the Tigers might have benefitted from the unsuccessful sacrifice because if they had ended up with runners at second and third then Royals manager Dick Howser would have likely instructed Quisenberry, a sinkerballer, to intentionally walk Johnny Grubb, a good low-ball hitter, to load the bases and pitch to Chet Lemon. As it stood, the Royals had to deal with Grubb, who subsequently stroked a two-run double to right field to give the Tigers a 5–3 lead.

As a broadcaster nothing quite feels as good as being right. After Grubb's hit I reiterated to a somewhat confused Howard why I thought the Tigers had lucked out by not successfully sacrificing the runners over. He cut me off and went on a long non-sequitur about how all the best sportswriters in America attended Ivy League schools. That pretty much clinched it: Howard was smashed.

The Tigers won the game to go up 2–0 in the best-of-five series. When the game ended, Al and I made a beeline to the press room. We both needed a drink. I asked the young woman behind the bar for a glass of wine, but Al decided to go with something stronger, a double shot of vodka on the rocks. The bartender took the bottle of Stoli and poured out half a shot. "Little light on the vodka there, huh?" Al protested.

The bartender hesitated before telling Al why he couldn't have two shots. "I'm sorry, Mr. Michaels," she said, "but your colleague drank the rest of the bottle."

On cue, Howard came stumbling in. He put his hands around Al and started up again with his accusation that Al never took a stance on anything. "You want me to take a stance?" Al replied angrily. "I'll take a stance, Howard. You embarrassed the network. You embarrassed Jim and me. And you certainly embarrassed yourself. Let's get out of here, Jim."

Outside, Al and I ran into one of our producers, Chuck Howard. "What's going on?" Chuck asked Al, who was visibly irritated by the evening's events.

"What's going on?" Al spit back. "You're the producer. How do you let a guy get completely blitzed in our booth in the middle of a playoff game?"

Howard joined us for the ride back to the Alameda Plaza Hotel. For several minutes nobody said a word. Then Curt Gowdy Sr., Howard's longtime friend who had broadcast the game for ABC Radio, finally broke the silence. "Howard, I've known you for 35 years," he said, shaking his head in obvious disapproval. "Why do you do this?"

The next day we flew to Detroit for what would end up being the clinching game of the series for the Tigers. The hijinks in the booth during Game 2 didn't escape the notice of the sportswriters. Dick Young, the longtime *New York Daily News* writer who antagonized Howard by referring to him as "Howie the Fraud" and other pejoratives, had a column about dissension between Cosell and Michaels. I'm not sure how much Howard remembered about the previous night, but when he found out about Young's column, he went to Al the next morning and offered the closest thing he had to an apology. "They're talking about dissension in the ABC booth," Howard said. "Alfalfa, tonight, you and I will be like long-lost brothers."

In the world according to Howard, it was like nothing had ever happened.

If people took Howard seriously or reacted to how rude he could be, he would have risked getting punched out on a daily basis. No one was safe around him. He groped flight attendants, bullied limo drivers, and tried to intimidate colleagues. Working with Howard obviously required a lot of patience and self-control. But we had a job to do. And it took a team of professionals, in front of and behind the camera, to make sure we delivered on our mission of informing and entertaining viewers who chose to spend a few hours with us on a summer or fall night. Take the game I just talked about. It could have turned into an absolute nightmare, but except for some tell-tale signs that Howard was in no condition to be appearing on live television, we managed to pull it off with minimal public embarrassment. That night featured Howard at his most extreme. But in general I don't think anybody fooled themselves into thinking that he was a team player.

When all is said and done, did Howard enhance or detract from the product? Howard went out of his way to be a polarizing figure, so it really depends on who you ask. Howard might have thought he was bigger than ABC Sports, but he wasn't. In 1985 he wrote an autobiography that criticized pretty much everybody at the network, especially his *Monday Night Football* colleagues Gifford and Meredith. As Al said at the time, "The book is full of venom from top to bottom, which is just how Howard has become of late." The network felt it could no longer tolerate Howard's conduct and announced that he wouldn't work the 1985 World Series. He spent the last years of his life and career back at the place he started, ABC Radio.

I'm sure most of you reading this book know the challenges of working with a difficult colleague. Now you know I can relate. While I learned a lot from Howard and admired him for the work he was capable of doing, I also always had to be on my guard when sitting next to him. But if you work for an organization whose mission you believe in, you will find a way to thrive. That's how I looked at it during my playing and broadcasting careers. With Earl Weaver I always knew the end game: getting to the World Series. And most years the Orioles fielded teams capable of winning a lot of games. Other than by looking at ratings, which say more about the popularity of an event than the appeal of the commentators, it's harder to judge the performance of broadcasters. But I think we did a pretty good job of delivering baseball games to homes across America in the 1980s.

I had the best of both worlds in the 1980s, broadcasting national games for ABC and local ones for a Baltimore audience. I'm proud to say that through the 2015 season I've worked on Orioles telecasts for 31 seasons, bringing my consecutive years of service with the team to half a century.

In the post-Howard Cosell era, Al, Tim McCarver, and I settled into a nice rhythm in the booth with ABC Sports president Dennis Swanson and Curt Gowdy Jr., the primary producer of *Monday Night Baseball*, calling the shots behind the scenes. As someone who grew up in the broadcasting world, Curt had tremendous instincts and a true love for the profession. He was the first guy at ABC who took the time to break down my work and provide constructive criticism.

Before Curt my communication with producers usually ended with the final out of a Monday night game and didn't pick up again until the following week. Curt kept in touch during the week, so much so that it became a running joke between Tim and me. I'd get a call from Tim at around 10:00 AM on a Wednesday warning me not to answer my phone because Curt had just given him an earful about something he felt we could have done better. But Curt helped me improve my performance. He stressed the importance of not talking over pitches and gave me tips on how to work effectively in a three-man booth without interrupting my colleagues, a process that involves hand signals and reading each other's eyes.

Except for the moments at the start of a game when we appeared on-camera to introduce ourselves and the event, my broadcast partners and I were pretty much heard but not seen. Tim referred to the opening

Out of necessity, more than ambition, veterans of the sportswriting fraternity have learned to broaden their horizons and expand their repertoires. In most cases this expansion of skills is prompted by impending college tuitions or perhaps kitchen renovations. Those of us who got into the newspaper business, interviewing players and filing game stories from press boxes inadvertently wandered into fields of broadcasting, book-writing, and public speaking because there was new demand for our voices, and we needed the supplementary income. People would ask me how I paid for my kids to go to Harvard, Boston University, and Boston College, and I'd answer, "That's why there are so many books."

We get to go on TV and radio and write books and speak to dental conventions because Americans love sports, and there is hunger for opinions and stories from those who have been behind the scenes. In the old days, our employers discouraged this outside work because we were spreading ourselves too thin and sharing intellectual property. Today, the bosses love our outside work because we are "spreading our brand," generating more clicks and followers. Career diversification is not for everybody. I see too many great doctors who gravitate to administration. We didn't need Bob Dylan to go electric. But for most of us who eventually lose our fastballs, it can be healthy and rewarding to try something new.
—DAN SHAUGHNESSY,
THE BOSTON GLOBE COLUMNIST
AND AUTHOR OF 12 BOOKS

segments of a game as "the 45 seconds of terror." It takes practice to figure out what to do with your body when the camera is trained so closely on you in a live setting. But I realized that if I wanted to make it in television broadcasting, I would need to become more comfortable in those situations. Sitting in a darkened studio or home and interviewing guests like I did in 1985 for a New York public television show called *The Sporting Life*, a 10-part series on the lives of athletes, helped me take that next step. I got good reviews from *The New York Times* critic, who called me "an engaging host, as appealing on television as representatives Jack Kemp, the old Buffalo Bill, or Bill Bradley, the old New York Knick." That made me sound more like an aspiring politician than a sportscaster, but it could have been a lot worse, I guess.

My contract with ABC allowed the network to use my services for events other than baseball. That was fine by me. I knew enough about golf, basketball, and tennis to be able to hold my own as a sideline reporter or commentator. ABC producers had more exotic assignments in mind for me, however. And that's how I ended up in Oberstdorf, West Germany, as a play-by-play announcer for the 1987 Ski Jumping World Cup. As many of you remember, *ABC's Wide World of Sports*, which aired from 1961 to 1998, was known for "spanning the globe to bring you the constant variety of sports." I felt honored to be a part of this legendary program. I just wished I knew something, anything, about ski jumping.

I remember flying over to Germany on a red-eye Lufthansa flight and being awakened in the morning by a Teutonic flight attendant announcing, "Ve vill now get up!" The experience was a little different than flying British Airways or Air Italia. But our lodgings more than made up for the brusque treatment from the Lufthansa flight crew. The Sonnenalp Resort in nearby Ofterschwang was beautiful. Before the start of the ski jumping competition, the ABC crew, their families, and I went cross country skiing. That group included actress Anne Archer, who was married to our producer, Terry Jastrow. Unfortunately, a day after we arrived, another producer had to rush back to the United States with his wife, who needed an appendectomy and preferred to have one in an American hospital.

My body had a hard time adjusting to the European time zone. I didn't sleep well. And I was nervous about the job that I had to do. To this point I had only worked as a color commentator on baseball games. I had never done play-by-play for anything in my life. In this case Jeff Hastings, an American ski jumper who participated in the 1984 Winter Olympics, would be filling the role of color guy.

We started reporting the story at 11:00 AM local time, which was 5:00 AM New York time. That gave us about 12 hours to put a 21-minute story together for that afternoon's *Wide World of Sports*. In a surprise result, Czechoslovakian Pavel Ploc outjumped Oberstdorf native Andreas Bauer to win the World Cup. Terry worked feverishly in the production truck to splice together highlights and to prepare us for what we needed to do to convey the drama of the event to American viewers whose only real exposure to ski jumping was "the agony of defeat" they saw each week in the opening credits of *Wide World of Sports*.

We worked all day to create a 21-minute broadcast—only to find out that the basketball game that preceded our segment ran long. Just like that, 21 minutes were cut to four. And instead of sending a mostly pre-taped segment over to New York, we received instructions that we were going live.

At 10:30 PM in Oberstdorf, Jeff Hastings and I stood on a small stage in the middle of an Alpine snowstorm waiting for word that studio host Frank Gifford was ready to hear from us. The snow was melting the scotch tape we used to fasten microphones to our suits. We had no monitor to see what was taking place in the New York studio. I heard the opening music and then heard Frank say, "Hey, Jim, it's Frank Gifford. Long time, no see." Then I heard our production assistant say to us, "I think we're on."

Terry hit the wrong button in the truck. The viewers at home didn't see the winning jump. They saw a losing jump. We didn't know that, though. When Jeff and I went on air, we stumbled through a recap of the day's events. Talk about the agony of defeat. It was a total disaster. Back at the hotel, I got a call from Curt Gowdy Jr., who oversaw *Wide World of Sports*. "How's it going, hoss?" Curt asked.

"I've had better days," I replied.

"Well, look at it this way, hoss," he said, "it can't get any worse than this."

In the ABC baseball broadcast booth in the mid-80s, my repartee with Earl continued. One of the times we worked with McCarver, Earl noticed that Tim's pregame meal was a bit light. Earl stared daggers though Tim's salad. "I'm on a diet, Earl," Tim said.

"You look emaciated."

"I want to look like Palmer."

"No one looks like Palmer. Eat a fucking potato, will ya!"

I guess this is as opportune a time as any to talk about my physical appearance. I'll be the first to admit that my looks certainly didn't hurt my career. In fact, they were at least partly responsible for taking my career to new places when I became a spokesman for Jockey International, a relationship that lasted 20 years.

We live in a beauty-obsessed world, and I heard references to my matinee-idol looks for my entire career. Baseball historian Bill James once said of me, "Jim Palmer was the ultimate pretty-boy athlete. Unnaturally handsome with clear blue eyes and a square, smiling face, he was also highly intelligent and articulate." At some point my looks threatened to become as much of a conversation topic as my fastball. An early Cal Ripken Jr. scouting report produced by the Pittsburgh Pirates referred to Cal as "Jim Palmer handsome." Forget about winning 268 games and three Cy Young awards, in many people's eyes I was just a pretty face. Again, that carries certain advantages. According to a University of Texas study, a handsome man stands to earn 13 percent more during his career than a less attractive peer. With that in mind, let's remember that beauty is in the eye of the beholder. I believe that people who exude confidence and present themselves well have a greater likelihood of being successful.

Would I have had the opportunity to appear in underwear commercials if I didn't look good in briefs? Probably not. But my history with Jockey was built more on loyalty than looks. I got my start with the Kenosha, Wisconsin-based company in 1977, the first year I took part in a print ad campaign that gave the American public a glimpse at what I and seven other athletes, including Pete Rose and Steve Carlton, looked like in our underwear. In 1976 Jockey did an ad campaign with a different group of athletes that advised men to look their best while wearing their least. The tagline for the '77 campaign, "Take Away Their Uniforms and Who Are They," wasn't posed as a question because the answer was plain to see. They put me in the skimpiest briefs of all at the New York City shoot.

I earned $3,500 for that first ad and I think Jockey felt like it got its money's worth. The cost of my Amtrak ticket from Baltimore to New York was $35. And I stayed only one night at the Hilton in Midtown Manhattan. Pete, on the other hand, missed a flight from Atlanta, forcing Jockey to spend $5,000 to charter a plane for him. I think that severely damaged Pete's relationship with the company, though the way he looked in his underwear may have also contributed to the end of his modelling days. Thank God he could hit.

In 1978 I was the only athlete from the previous year's shoot who got invited to endorse Jockey again. This time it was with three other athletes: Lydell Mitchell of the Baltimore Colts, Marques Johnson of the Milwaukee Bucks, and Shep Messing, a goaltender for the Oakland Stompers soccer team. That ad had a real classic 1970s look. The photographer took a burst of images, creating a strobe effect that showed me in various stages of my pitching motion. To get the action shot just right, I threw a baseball into a blanket about 50 times.

All of the Jockey ads were ahead of their time—groundbreaking—even. Bill Herrmann, the company's vice president of sales, calculated that women made 75 percent of men's underwear purchases. So in an attempt to appeal to the majority of the underwear-buying public without alienating the underwear-wearing public, he devised a plan to target each group at a personal and emotional level. When Jockey decided to go with a single face for the campaign, Herrmann set out to find the athlete who he thought men found most relatable and women found easiest on the eyes.

In today's world Jockey probably would have conducted an online poll to determine which athlete would earn the right to star in future campaigns. Back then, companies relied on old-fashioned market research to decide who would most ably represent their products. They narrowed the field of candidates down to two: me and Steve Garvey of the Dodgers. They took us around to shopping malls and counted the number of people who showed up. And they conducted popularity tests to see who scored highest. Finally, they had us both do a photo shoot with famed photographer Harold Krieger at his New York studio. Krieger was a real pro who had shot covers for *Life* and *Look* magazines. When Jockey's executives analyzed all the information, they decided I was the right man for the job. Krieger's photos became the basis for several more ads.

A lot of people over the years have asked me what it was like being a sex symbol. I start by telling them that without Harold Krieger, I might not have reached that status. When I saw the photos he took, I hardly recognized myself. That's not me being self-deprecating. It's a true statement about the magic of lighting and studio photography.

As the face of Jockey, I branched out into television ads. I found that exciting because it had been years since I had shot a commercial. In the early 1970s, I appeared in a commercial for Brylcream, a popular hair care product of the era ("A little dab will do ya") that was shot over a two-day period in Miami—one day at a ballpark and the other on a boat sailing across Biscayne Bay. Check it out on YouTube if you'd like.

During the 1980s I did about 20 to 25 store appearances a year for Jockey across the country. Each of those days consisted of radio or television appearances in the morning, autograph sessions at the stores in the afternoon, and meetings with buyers later in the day. Jockey hit on a really winning formula. Husbands and wives would show up together to the store appearances. Women bought Jockey because they liked the ads. At the same time, their husbands didn't feel threatened by the man in the ad. In fact they felt completely comfortable telling me how much their wives enjoyed seeing me in my underwear. I don't think they would have said that to a regular model, but they had no qualms about sharing that with a baseball player who was moonlighting as a model. On a visit to New York, I ran into Bill Farley, the head of Union Underwear—then the largest underwear company in the world. Bill told me that despite his company having a much larger market share than Jockey, everyone seemed to think Jockey was king. It meant a lot to me to see a little company with local ownership become such a major name and competitor in the industry.

My teammates got a kick out of my side project. They had seen me in my skivvies hundreds of times and couldn't understand what the fuss was all about. Scott McGregor tells a story of how a woman in an Orioles cap excitedly approached him in the Memorial Stadium parking lot during the 1977 season. *Wow*, Scotty thought, *I haven't been with the club long, but I already have fans.*

"Oh, my friends won't believe I met you," the woman gushed. "Can I please have your autograph, Mr. Palmer?"

"Mr. Palmer? Do I look like a model?" Scotty said laughing.

In my work for Jockey, I applied the same level of preparation as I did on the baseball field. I drew from my experiences and learned from them. And I worked hard to represent the company to the best of my ability. I showed up on time, never missed a store appearance, and kept myself in shape. It's not a coincidence that I spent as many years pitching Jockey underwear as I did pitching baseballs for the Orioles. Both were companies I respected. It's amazing to think that a $35 train ticket from Baltimore to New York turned into a 20-year affiliation with Jockey.

My business ties with The Money Store and Nutramax Laboratories started similarly and led to long-term relationships based on mutual trust and admiration. In the 1990s I was in Sacramento, California, speaking at an event aimed at encouraging local businesses to hire special-needs people. The Money Store, the largest private employer in California's capital city at that time, helped sponsor a luncheon. Afterward, Marc Turteltaub, the company's president, requested to meet with me. A couple of weeks later over breakfast in Baltimore, he offered me an opportunity to endorse the company's line of mortgages and home equity loans. I followed in the footsteps of Phil Rizzuto, whose "Holy Cow!" ads for The Money Store became classics.

My longtime affiliation with Nutramax was born out of a genuine belief that its Cosamin Joint Health Supplement can help joint pain sufferers maintain an active lifestyle well into their senior years. It goes without saying that my body took a beating during a long athletic career. In addition to throwing baseballs for a living, I've always run and played tennis and golf in my free time. The thought of not being able to do those things in my post-retirement years scared me. But when your knees go, your athletic options become limited. Even everyday activities become difficult. By my 50s I had no cartilage left in my knee. It was bone on bone, and I appeared a likely candidate for knee replacement surgery. The Cosamin really made a difference in my life. I avoided surgery (knock on wood) and am still doing the outdoor activities that are a key part of what makes me happy and who I am. I believe in Nutramax's products and I love the fact that Nutramax is Maryland-based and committed to the betterment of the area. It's the people behind the brands that attract me to a company. At Nutramax Dr. Robert Henderson and his son, Troy, are passionate about what they do and treat their customers, employees, and community well.

In order to lead a fulfilling life after my playing career ended, I had to go outside of my comfort zone. I never in a million years thought I would ever pose in my skivvies on a billboard in Times Square or broadcast a ski jump competition in the middle of a snowstorm in the German Alps. But I'm glad I seized on those opportunities.

VISIT TO THE MOUND

Dan Schwabel, who writes about workplace issues for *Time* and *Forbes*, says we're living in an "age of diversification" where balancing multiple jobs is an increasing necessity. "In the age of

I display my Cy Young award in 1976. It was the second consecutive year I earned what is considered an individual award, but it was really due to a team effort. (AP Images)

Mike Flanagan and I are in the Memorial Stadium locker room during the 1979 World Series. It was hard not to smile when Flanny was around. (AP Images)

From left to right, Cincinnati Bengals quarterback Ken Anderson, myself, and St. Louis Cardinals quarterback Jim Hart pose for a Jockey underwear advertisement in 1977. (AP Images)

I served as a spokesman and model for Jockey for 20 years. (Jockey International, Inc.)

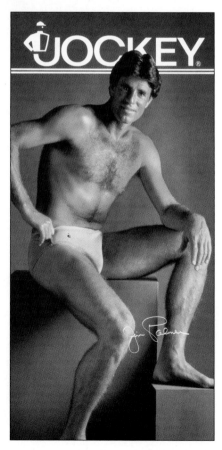

My father, Max, receives Little League Parent of the Year from Dr. Creighton Hale in Williamsport, Pennsylvania, in 1984. (Courtesy Jim Palmer)

I am honored at Jim Palmer Day at Memorial Stadium on September 1, 1985. (Courtesy Jim Palmer)

I have been fortunate to broadcast Orioles games since the 1980s.

Nowadays, my office is basically in the broadcast booth at baseball stadiums.

Before a game I talk with Orioles hitting coach Scott Coolbaugh. I interact with Orioles coaches and managers so that I keep my finger on the pulse of the game. (Courtesy Jim Palmer)

Broadcasting baseball games is an enjoyable livelihood, but it takes a lot of preparation and hard work.

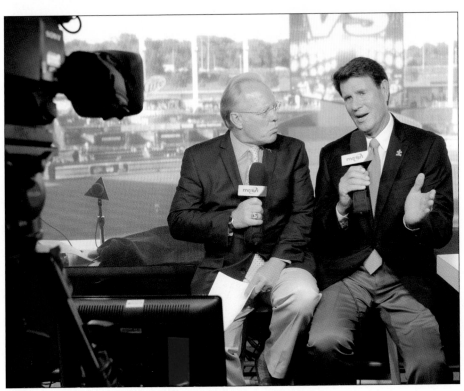

After all of that prep work, my broadcasting partner Gary Thorne and I go on the air before a game at Kauffman Stadium in Kansas City, Missouri.

I throw in a spring training game on March 11, 1991, as part of a comeback attempt at age 45. A torn hamstring would thwart my ambitious effort. (AP Images)

When I was in high school, I was very uncomfortable in front of the microphone, but through hard work, I now pride myself on my public speaking skills.

I am proud to have been inducted into the Hall of Fame in 1990 with Joe Morgan, who incidentally led off the 1977 All-Star Game with a home run off me.

I stand next to my plaque during my induction into the National Baseball Hall of Fame in 1990.

I am blessed to have two beautiful daughters, Kelly (left) and Jamie (right). (Courtesy Jim Palmer)

I am with my wife and stepson after the last All-Star Game at Yankee Stadium. I was happy to share that 2008 moment with Susan and Spencer. (Courtesy Jim Palmer)

diversification, you need to have multiple sources of income and the best way to accomplish that is by having an entrepreneurial mind-set," Schnabel writes. "Think about career diversification the same way you think about managing a portfolio of stocks. If you put all of your money on one stock and it plummets, you are broke and living with your parents. On the other hand, if you invest in a series of stocks across various industries, you are more balanced and if one tanks you can stay afloat."

It's normal, even admirable, to feel loyalty to an employer who treats you well and provides you with a job opportunity that you find fulfilling. The act of seeking out work to do on the side is enough to make someone feel like an unfaithful spouse. But work isn't marriage. We live in an uncertain world, and it behooves us to give ourselves as many options as possible. Assuming that it's possible and permissible given your current workload and the rules of your workplace, I recommend at least exploring the possibility of side projects that can be completed on your own time. Be sensible. You don't want your freelance or contract assignments to interfere with your dedication to your full-time job. On the other hand, you don't want to get caught flat-footed if your company suddenly downsizes and you find yourself in need of income and contacts.

Ask yourself: am I looking to switch careers or do I just want to scratch an itch and take on side projects that allow me to use my talents in a different way? If you're contemplating a career change, start by compiling a list of your transferable skills. Be ready to show how the skills you've developed in your current line of work would apply to a new career path. Writing for Entrepeneur.com, Deborah Mitchell, the CEO of Deborah Mitchell Media Associates, offered the following four-pronged strategy for people looking to make midlife career changes: take time to regroup, assess your skills, invest in education, and gather your success team. Preparing yourself for a career change makes taking a leap into the unknown a lot less frightening.

7ᵗʰ Inning Stretch

I LOVE THE GAME OF BASEBALL AND FEEL INDEBTED TO the Orioles organization for nurturing my ability, hiring some of the best baseball minds around, and surrounding me with teammates who helped make me better. More than 30 years after I pitched my last game for the O's, the club's well-being remains extremely important to me. So before we get to the last two "innings" of the book that deal with appreciation and having fun, I want to share a few more anecdotes about my time in Baltimore.

Because this is the seventh inning stretch, I have to tip my cap to Orioles fans, who off and on for decades have belted out the John Denver song "Thank God I'm a Country Boy," immediately following the more staid and traditional "Take Me Out to the Ballgame." Denver himself performed the song on the top of our dugout before Game 1 of the 1983 World Series. It's a great tradition that pre-dates Boston Red Sox fans crooning "Sweet Caroline." O's fans don't get nearly enough credit for their innovation, energy, and passion. So for those of you familiar with the tune, I'd like to say, "Yee Haw!"

A lot of people over the years have asked if I've ever considered working for the Orioles in a capacity other than broadcaster. It's a reasonable question, considering that the Orioles have had 14 different skippers since I played my final game in 1984. But the answer is: no, I've never seriously entertained the idea of making myself a candidate for a managerial, coaching, or front-office position. I have, however, been approached several times over the years by Orioles majority owner Peter Angelos about managing the club. Let me start by saying that I really admire Peter for his commitment to the organization and his belief in me. Although the club hasn't enjoyed the level of success that we became accustomed to during my playing career, Peter is always looking for ways to field a winning team. He cares about the team and he cares about the community. When he bought the Orioles, he compared it to the Chesapeake Bay, calling it a national treasure.

Peter first gauged my level of interest in the job in 1993, the year his group bought the team for $173 million. Johnny Oates was managing the team at the time. Peter reached out to me through David Bernstein, the chairman of the Duty Free Company and a limited partner in the team, who happened to be a neighbor of mine. David came over and told me Peter wanted to have lunch with me. Who doesn't like lunch? So I told David to tell Peter that I would be happy to dine with him. The following week I met Peter at a great little Italian restaurant in Baltimore called Bocaccio's. I had no clue what Peter wanted to discuss and figured he just wanted to get to know the organization's history better through me. But from the time the waiter poured water into our glasses, Peter made it clear that he came to talk about the job Johnny was doing. "I listen to your broadcasts," he told me. "How is it that you know what's going on, but the manager doesn't?"

The question surprised me. It's not like the Orioles were playing poorly at the time. They were 11 games over .500, in fact. I didn't really see why he would go after Johnny, who had led a team with a pretty mediocre roster to 89 wins the previous season. "I put a lot of preparation into my broadcasts," I responded, "but at the end of the day, I've yet to lose one up there."

Peter had more to get off his chest. He groused about how Johnny didn't handle reporters well, a shortcoming that had greater significance in the pre-Washington Nationals era, when the glare of the Metroplex media shone much brighter on the Orioles. That had some merit. But Johnny was a Cal Ripken Sr. disciple who knew the game as well as anyone. He just wasn't comfortable with the media. That was no reason to fire him, especially considering Peter didn't have anyone in mind to succeed him. I suggested Peter hire a media consultant to help Johnny navigate those sometimes choppy waters. I also told him that he would benefit from meeting the players, many of whom probably thought of him as just some rich lawyer in a suit who made a fortune representing plaintiffs in lawsuits. "Show them you care about the game, the organization, and about them," I advised.

The next day, David called me to say how much Peter enjoyed our lunch. "He wants to know if you want to be general manager or manager," David informed me. "It's your choice."

"No, David," I replied. "I want to have lunch with Peter once a year to talk about the organization, but that's it. I know my boundaries."

Peter would return to the subject of me managing the team in the 1990s. After the Orioles fired Phil Regan in 1995, he asked me if I had any interest in the job. I again politely declined. And I felt that Peter made an excellent choice when he instead hired my former teammate Davey Johnson, who, as skipper of the New York Mets, showed he could lead a team to a title.

That year, in the midst of a wild-card race, Peter called and asked me what I thought of two of the team's most recent acquisitions, Bobby Bonilla and David Wells. I told him the truth as I saw it. Bonilla didn't run balls out and seemed like a complainer. He had skills and wasn't a bad guy, but I didn't think he represented "The Oriole Way." Neither did David Wells, I told Peter. I realized that from the moment David first rolled in on his motorcycle to Orioles spring training. "Hey, David," I said, "welcome to the O's. Let me know if there's anything you need."

"Who do you know in San Diego?" he fired back.

The 1996 season hadn't even started, but David was already thinking of his chances of landing with the Padres as a free agent in October. I told him I knew Larry Lucchino pretty well from his time as Orioles president. Larry had left Baltimore to take the same job in San Diego. "Have a good year, David," I told him. "If you end up a free agent, I'll make a call for you."

The Wells-Orioles relationship seemed doomed from the start. David liked motorcycles, tattoos, and tank tops. He was a redneck in Baltimore. More importantly, he was a fly ball pitcher at Camden Yards, a home-run park. David went 11–14 with a 5.14 ERA in '96. He signed as a free agent with the New York Yankees at the end of the season. He pitched a perfect game in New York and eventually found his way to sunny San Diego in 2004. Boomer moved around a lot but had a nice career, winning 239 games. He just wasn't a good fit in Baltimore.

During Davey's tenure as skipper, Peter got annoyed that Davey didn't keep him in the loop on matters pertaining to the team. I hoped they could put their personal differences aside because under Davey the team flourished, making back-to-back trips to the American League Championship Series in his first two years managing the team.

But the beginning of the end for Davey came after he fined Roberto Alomar $10,500 in July 1997 for skipping out on an exhibition game against Triple A Rochester. Several other players missed the game with pre-approved excuses, but Alomar didn't tell Davey, general manager Pat Gillick, or anyone else in a position of authority that he would be a no-show. I don't think Peter had a problem with Davey fining Alomar, but it greatly upset him that Davey directed Alomar to pay the fine to a charity at Johns Hopkins University for which Davey's wife had raised funds. In November of 1997, Davey resigned as manager just hours before he received the American League Manager of the Year award from the baseball writers.

I think it used to be a lot simpler to manage a major league team. Or maybe "straightforward" is a better word. When I started my career in 1965, the amount of money a player received for being on a championship-winning team often exceeded his annual salary. My World Series share in 1966 was $11,682.04. My salary that season was $7,500. Nowadays, there isn't a real financial incentive for players to make it to the postseason. In 2015 Clayton Kershaw earned $30 million, making him the highest-paid player in the majors. In my rookie year of 1965, Willie Mays topped that list when he earned just a shade over $100,000. I hope players are motivated as much by pride as by money, but I'm not sure that's always the case. The age of long-term, guaranteed contracts adds an additional layer of difficulty to a manager's job. How do you get the most out of a player who will make millions of dollars regardless of his performance? I hesitate to start too many sentences with, "Back when I played..." because it makes me sound both old and envious, but I think we can learn something from how baseball used to be. So here goes: back when I played, you had to win 20 games to get a $20,000 raise. Baseball functioned much more like the rest of the world, where businesses provide incentives for performance and reward workers for achieving goals. A car salesman who doesn't sell cars isn't going to last very long in that line of work. I'm not saying the pay-for-performance model doesn't have flaws, but generally speaking, I believe people, even those who take great pride in their work, will work harder and more efficiently if financial or other incentives are offered.

It used to be that managers could get away with being miserable dictators. Not anymore. The balance of power has shifted completely to the players, who hold the fate of managers in their hands. If a team underachieves, a manager loses his job. It's much easier to fire a manager than to fire 25 players. So if I'm ever asked again if I'd consider managing the team, the answer will still be no.

* * *

As my career went on, I became more and more known as a control pitcher. And to the extent that I couldn't get by on speed alone and didn't try to intimidate hitters with high and tight fastballs, the label fit. My strategy for keeping hitters off balance involved mixing up my pitches. Earl Weaver approved of that gameplan. Pitchers who come in on hitters are sooner or later going to provoke a response from opposing pitchers. Earl detested the idea of beanball wars for the simple reason that he didn't want to risk losing any of his players to injury. We had a pitcher named Grant Jackson, whom Earl would chastise for brushing back hitters. "Look around," he'd say. "Is our third baseman better than theirs? How about our left fielder? We can beat this team with the players we have on the field. I don't want anyone to get hurt."

I hit 38 batters during my career, an average of only two a season. And only twice in my career did I intentionally throw at a hitter—once to try and knock him down and the other time to hit him. Let's start with the former. In 1979 U.L. Washington of the Kansas City Royals, he of toothpick-always-in-the-mouth fame, did enough in my opinion to warrant a pitch under the chin. It was a hot afternoon in Kansas City, and my elbow hurt like hell. I threw him a change-up that he must have been expecting because when he swung and missed, his face contorted into a pained grimace. I could tell he was thinking, *How in the world did I miss that pitch?* That might not seem like enough of a provocation to throw a purpose pitch, but between the pain in my arm, the heat of the day, the stupid toothpick in U.L.'s mouth, and his reaction to missing the pitch, I felt moved to send a message. I needed a couple of tries to get a

There are several theories about the origin of the seventh-inning stretch—probably the most popular being that the tradition began on April 14, 1910, when then-president William Howard Taft rose out of his seat in the middle of the seventh inning of a baseball game between the Washington Senators and the Philadelphia A's to stretch his 6'2", 350-pound frame. The fans in attendance felt obliged to follow the president's lead, and thus a tradition was born.

As this tradition applies to my own lengthy career in baseball, I feel I'm in my personal version of the stretch. Fifteen seasons as a player, followed by 31 years in the broadcast booth, provides plenty of opportunity for reflection. Two-thirds of my playing career was with the Baltimore Orioles. Those 10 seasons were easily the most enjoyable of my playing career. During those years the O's won more regular-season games than any other team, averaging more than 90 wins a season. All that winning would help me define myself as a winner in baseball. In fact, during my 15-year career, only three other players played in more winning games than me: Pete Rose, Reggie Jackson, and Joe Morgan.

My second career in baseball also has had a winning edge. After 12 seasons broadcasting for the Montreal Expos, I joined the New York Yankees TV crew in 1997. The 2016 season represents my 21st year announcing Yankees games. The team hasn't had a losing season during my time in the booth.

When you get to this portion of your career, it's nice to look back at the people and things that helped get you to where you are. For me, that means thinking about my talented, never-give-up Orioles teammates and all of the creative TV colleagues I've worked alongside.
—KEN SINGLETON, FORMER MAJOR LEAGUE OUTFIELDER AND YANKEES BROADCASTER

fastball up and in on him. It was the closest I ever came to hitting someone in the head with a pitch. Fortunately, he avoided the ball by diving to the ground. When he popped back up, the thin shard of wood still protruded from his mouth. U.L. was a cool customer.

The other, more notorious time that I threw at a hitter came in 1976 after Dock Ellis of the New York Yankees beaned Reggie Jackson in the face with a fastball, resulting in Reggie leaving the field on a stretcher. After someone tried to bunt on Dock earlier in the game, he profanely informed those of us sitting in the home dugout that the next guy who attempted a bunt would get hit in the head. In response, Reggie got on the top step of the dugout and invited Dock to make him the target. Dock obliged in the bottom of the eighth inning, prompting Earl to make a rare exception to his no-beanball rule. "We can't let that happen," he told me before I went out to mound for the top of the ninth inning of a game we led 4–0. "Someone has to go down."

Elrod Hendricks, my former teammate, led off the inning for the Yankees. I didn't want to hit the guy who caught my only career no-hitter, so I spared him. After Elrod flied out to right, I set my sights on Mickey Rivers, a difficult target considering his propensity for darting and dancing in the batter's box like he had a severe case of jock itch. I finally nicked him with a fastball on the fourth pitch of the at-bat. He stole second and scored on a single. I admitted to reporters after the game that I plunked Rivers on purpose because we had to protect our players. American League president Lee MacPhail got wind of my comments and called the next morning to inform me I owed him $500. I managed to put off paying him until the start of the following season. A day before my scheduled Opening Day start, I got a telegram from MacPhail's office that read, "If you plan on pitching tomorrow, I need to get the $500."

It cost me $500 and a shutout to follow through on Earl's orders, but it was without a doubt the right thing to do.

Sometimes the threat of a beanball carried enough weight to get my message across. One night in the late 1970s, I was facing Jim Spencer, a Baltimore-area native and a friend of mine. There were only four players in my career whom I faced more than Jim, and I always handled him pretty well. At one point, he went hitless in 32 straight at-bats against me. I guess he felt desperate that night because after falling behind in the count 0–2, Jim tried to sneak a peek at the signs that Rick Dempsey was flashing me. Demper came out to the mound to let me know about Jim's chicanery. I stepped off of the mound and verbally tipped my next pitch to Jim: a fastball right at his head. I don't think I meant it, but it sounded good at the time. Then I stepped back on the rubber and threw a fastball...right down the middle of the plate for the third strike.

* * *

Of all the thousands of players I competed with or against or watched from the stands or a press box, none were more worthy of admiration than the great Yogi Berra, who passed away at the age of 90 in 2015.

A few years ago, my wife, Susan, and I ran into Yogi and his wife, Carmen, during a morning stroll through Cooperstown over Hall of Fame weekend. I always enjoyed my annual chats with Yogi and was thrilled that Susan was going to have a chance to meet one of my heroes. Now you have to understand something about Susan. She's from College Station, Texas, home to Texas A&M University. Football is a way of life down there, and with the exception of the kickers and punters, it's not difficult to identify who plays the game. So when Susan laid eyes on Yogi, she had no idea what to make of the diminutive Yankees legend. "So you got in the Hall of Fame for managing," she said to Yogi. "What teams did you manage?"

Now it's true that Yogi managed both the New York Yankees and Mets, leading each team to a pennant. But unbeknownst to my wife, he had also won three American League MVP awards and played on 10 World Series-winning teams, the most of anyone in history.

Yogi got a chuckle out of Susan's question. Even in his prime, he didn't exactly strike an imposing figure, but at 80-something, he was becoming increasingly frail. That's what made him special. He was Everyman. Whether helping to storm the beaches of Normandy in WWII or swatting three home runs in the 1956 World Series, he simply and unassumingly did his job in an exceptional manner.

Yogi grew up in the same St. Louis neighborhood as Joe Garagiola, who had a decent major league career but is better known for the broadcasting and game show hosting he did in his later years. Branch Rickey, who served as general manager of the St. Louis Cardinals before moving on to the Dodgers, knew that both Yogi and Joe wanted nothing more than to play for their hometown team. In Rickey's opinion Joe was the bigger talent, both literally and figuratively, so he offered him $500 to sign with the club in 1942. Rickey thought enough of Yogi to want to bring him on board, too, but he didn't want to pay him a penny more than $250 for his services. Seventeen-year-old Yogi told Rickey in so many words, "Thanks, but no thanks." To borrow a phrase he later made famous, Yogi didn't know where he was going, but he had the self-confidence to know that he might wind up somewhere else. And of course he did, in New York, where he signed with the Yankees for $500. Then he went off and fought in World War II, risking his life for a cause that he knew had far more importance than baseball.

Back on the homefront in 1946, Yogi made an immediate impact with the Yankees. My favorite thing about Yogi the player is that he never saw a pitch he didn't think he could hit. His 12 strikeouts in 656 plate appearances in 1950 is proof of that. Oh, by the way, he hit .322 that season. And that wasn't even one of his three MVP years. Take the World Series rings, the extraordinary class, the workman-like approach to his job, and add to it his involvement in the Yogi Berra Museum and Learning Center in Montclair, New Jersey, and you have a guy we should all aspire to emulate.

One year at the annual Hall of Fame dinner, I sat at a table with Yogi, Whitey Ford, Duke Snider, Willie Mays, and Tommy Lasorda. It might have been the greatest table ever. I just sat and listened to these legends tell stories. Willie, in his high-pitched voice, told me that I was one of the wildest pitchers he ever faced. Either he remembered my season at Single A ball in Aberdeen or he was mistaking me for someone else because I only faced him once in my career, striking him out in the 1970 All-Star Game.

During the salad course, Tommy told Yogi about how the Dodgers had recently honored him with Tommy Lasorda Day at Dodger Stadium. As part of the ceremony, the team presented him with a tombstone plaque that read, "Dodger Stadium was his address and every ballpark was his home." Tommy asked Yogi what he wanted inscribed on his tombstone. Between bites of salad, Yogi said, "That's easy, Tommy. *It's over.*"

On the day of the last game at the old Yankee Stadium, Yogi showed up with a slew of former Bronx Bombers to give the hallowed stadium a grand send-off. Part of the program involved a photo montage of deceased Yankees like Joe DiMaggio, Mickey Mantle, and Babe Ruth. Yogi, who was standing next to Don Mattingly, got choked up. "Jeez, Donnie, I sure hope I never see my picture up there," he said.

As Yogi famously said, "It ain't over 'til it's over." But when it's over, it's over. And that's incredibly sad.

* * *

Earl Weaver and I didn't have a perfect marriage. Far from it. We were always sniping at each other, and in especially tense times, I wondered if I really wanted to endure the aggravation of playing for the guy.

A game at Texas early in the 1978 season helped bring Earl and me to the brink of divorce. The person who almost broke us up: Rangers center fielder Juan Beniquez. I had a 2–0 lead in the sixth inning when Beniquez fought off a fastball on the inner-half of the plate and dunked a ball in for a run-scoring double. A Jim Sundberg single then tied the game.

Earl, who thought he knew more about pitching than anyone who ever lived, got in my face between innings, demanding to know why I hadn't thrown Beniquez a slider. Our 11–16 start to the season had put Earl in a particularly foul mood, but I didn't think he had any business questioning my pitch selection. By winning 20 or more games in seven of the past eight seasons, I felt I had earned the right not to be second-guessed. I felt I should be able to throw the pitches I wanted even if not all of them ended up getting hitters out. "Look, Earl, I'm doing the best I can," I shouted at him. "If you don't think that's true, then you can take me out and bring someone else in."

That made Earl even more furious. He accused me of quitting on the team, but he decided to keep me in the game anyway. I guess I took the emotion of the dugout dust-up with Earl out with me on the mound the next inning because I quickly loaded the bases with nobody out. Earl gave me the hook and brought Don Stanhouse in. Later in the inning, Beniquez came up again with the bases still loaded. By this time I was in the clubhouse icing my arm. But I heard what happened next on the radio. Stanhouse threw a slider that Beniquez smacked off the left-field wall for a two-run double. The runners that Stanhouse inherited from me came home, so I was on the hook for the loss. But at least Earl wasn't proven right.

After the game ended, I braced for the second round of my argument with Earl. I knew it was coming because I heard the clickety-clack sound of his tiny spikes as he ran down the hallway leading to the clubhouse. He saw me sitting in front of my locker and again accused me of quitting on the team. "You know what, Earl," I said, "maybe it's time for me to leave. Whatever I do, it's not good enough for you. All you do is complain and question me and now you're accusing me of *quitting on us*. Even you know that's ridiculous."

Earl just looked at me, seething before he retreated to his office. He emerged a while later to call an impromptu team meeting. "Who here wants to be traded?" he bellowed. My teammates hadn't heard his exchange with me, so they had no idea what prompted Earl's question. No one raised his hand, of course. Then Earl pointed at me. "Because *that* cocksucker doesn't want to be on this team!"

I kept my distance from Earl for the next three days, sitting out in the bullpen until he came to his senses and apologized to me. I don't think he ever uttered the words, "I'm sorry," but by the time of my next start, we had moved on to talking about facing the

Minnesota Twins. Fortunately, neither Beniquez nor anyone else was ever capable of splitting us up.

* * *

One of the keys to being a successful pitcher is getting the weaker hitters in a lineup out while limiting the damage that the big bats can inflict. I pitched to contact, tried not to hurt myself with walks, and avoided giving up runs in bunches.

Even when I was leading the American League in innings pitched, I never struck out more than 200 batters in a season. If I had a runner on third base with less than two outs, I tried to strike out a hitter, but otherwise, I tried to throw pitches that hitters couldn't square up and let my defense do its job. I had some great fielders behind me.

No pitcher likes to give up the longball. The act of watching a hitter trot around the bases after smashing a ball over the fence is unpleasant and bad for a stat line. I gave up 20 or more home runs in a season seven times, but I didn't let that high number get to me. Nine of Jim Rice's 19 career hits off of me were homers, but I could live with that because eight of them were solo shots. As I mentioned earlier, I went through my entire major league career without yielding a grand slam. The Jim Rices of the world were going to get their licks in, but as long as only they rounded the bases after taking me deep, I knew I could keep my team in most games.

As two of the top players of the era, Rice and I had a friendly rivalry between the lines. Off the field, we got a chance to know each other in a less adversarial setting when we attended annual events sponsored by Spalding, whose equipment we both used. But old antagonisms never quite die, I guess. A couple of years ago, after I criticized Red Sox slugger David Ortiz during an Orioles broadcast for arguing balls and strikes, Jim told the Boston media that I should "quit complaining and let the guys go out and play."

Some hitters are going to give you trouble no matter what you do. Rod Carew was a perfect example. I first faced Rod in the Florida

Instructional League in 1964. At the time I had no way of knowing that he would go on to win seven American League batting titles, but he gave an early glimpse of what he could do when he took the best curveball I threw that fall and deposited into left field for a single. Rod simply played the game at a different level, making it all the more important to get out the guys who hit around him. He was one of the best contact hitters of all time, which meant he could bunt for a base hit with two strikes and seemingly put the ball anywhere on the field that he wanted. Rod hit a robust .352 off of me in his career, the highest average of any player who faced me more than 100 times. At .286 Reggie Jackson had the second highest average of that group.

Including Reggie and Rod, here are nine members of the Hall of Fame whom I faced 50 or more times in my career: Jim Rice (.218), Carl Yastrzemski (.243), Robin Yount (.267), George Brett (.342), Harmon Killebrew (.133), Luis Aparicio (.246), and Al Kaline (.217). The moral of the story: good pitching beats good hitting...sometimes.

* * *

At their best, sporting events provide viewers with great entertainment and a welcome escape from stresses of daily life and turmoil of the world. Every so often, however, athletic competitions turn into important global news. The 1972 Summer Olympics in Munich offered a tragic example with Jim McKay of ABC Sports taking on the role of lead anchor when armed Palestinian terrorists stormed a building that housed the delegation of Israeli athletes, taking hostages and ultimately killing 11 athletes and coaches. Jim's ability to guide viewers through the harrowing 16-hour ordeal was a tribute to his journalistic ability. The situation in Munich unfolded long before the days of round-the-clock cable news networks and their parade of correspondents and pundits, so the pressure fell squarely on Jim to tell the story and to tell it right. And he did so with tact, confidence, and skill. When the live drama came to its nightmare conclusion, Jim delivered the somber news unscripted: "We've just gotten final word...Our worst fears have been realized tonight.

They have now said there were 11 hostages. Two were killed in their rooms yesterday morning. Nine were killed at the airport tonight. They're all gone."

I felt proud to be affiliated with a network that included the likes of Jim McKay, whose name will forever be associated with the grace in how he handled the horrific tragedy. I also feel lucky to have worked with Al Michaels and Tim McCarver. Although none of us experienced the type of horror that happened in Munich, we did take part in guiding viewers through the worst natural disaster to take place during a game.

The 1989 World Series, the first ever "Battle of the Bay" between the San Francisco Giants and Oakland A's, had plenty of great storylines without the one that ended up defining it. Oakland had the "Bash Brothers"—Jose Canseco and Mark McGwire—and tremendous starting pitching. The Giants had Will "The Thrill" Clark and National League MVP Kevin Mitchell. And the setting couldn't have been better for us. Not only was the Bay Area one of the most beautiful places in the world, the matchup meant our crew only had to cross a bridge to get from one stadium to the other.

Behind great outings from Dave Stewart and Mike Moore, the A's jumped out to a 2–0 lead in the series. At that point I think all of us, including our families and crew, were hoping the Giants would climb back into the series so that we could maximize the amount of time we had in Northern California. On the travel day between Games 2 and 3, we got to fully enjoy our surroundings. My then-wife Joni and I spent the day browsing the stores at Union Square. Along the way Joni ran into some die-hard Giants and A's fans looking to attend Game 3, so she dipped into the allotment of tickets I had received to make a few extra bucks. That night the entire ABC team and our wives descended on Al's favorite restaurant, Trader Vic's, for Polynesian food and drinks. It was a rare Monday night during the NFL season that Al wasn't off broadcasting an NFL game. ABC didn't think it was feasible for him to fly cross country to Buffalo for that night's game and then have him return to San Francisco on Tuesday for the next World Series game, so Frank Gifford handled the play-by-play duties for the Los Angeles Rams-Buffalo Bills game that night.

We had a wonderful time at the restaurant. And Joni won everyone's hearts when the bill came and she threw down a wad of $100 bills, her spoils from the ticket sales.

That turned out to be the proverbial quiet before the storm. Looking back, everything seemed just a little out of sync when the sun rose on Tuesday morning. Al, who could do no wrong at ABC, woke up to an angry phone call from ABC Sports president Dennis Swanson. It stemmed from an exchange Al and I had during Sunday night's game when, after one of our several promos for *Monday Night Football*, I turned to Al and asked him what time we should be in his hotel room on Monday night. "For what?" he asked.

"For compulsory viewing of *Monday Night Football*," I said.

"We'll VCR it," Al responded.

Swanson took Al to task for blowing the opportunity to yet again talk up the football game. "Palmer threw you the perfect touchdown pass in the end zone, and you dropped it," Dennis told him.

Maybe Al had dropped the ball on that one, but considering how few miscues he made, it was forgivable. Dennis' football analogy, though, was appropriate, considering that ABC's priorities had shifted away from baseball. In fact 1989 was the last year of the network's contract with Major League Baseball, making our work on the World Series that much more important to us.

At Tuesday morning's production meeting, we went over the plan for that evening's broadcast. On-field reporter Joe Morgan was scheduled to do a pregame interview with Giants legend Willie Mays. With punctuality always being a concern with Willie, producer Curt Gowdy Jr. discussed a contingency plan in case Willie showed up late or not at all. As the meeting dragged on, McCarver sat there white as a sheet in the grips of a 24-hour flu bug.

October 17, 1989, was an unusually warm day in San Francisco, somewhere around 84 degrees with very little wind. I was sweltering in my dark blazer. Fortunately, Willie showed up early for his chat with Joe, so we didn't have to improvise an entire segment.

Networks try to leave nothing to chance when it comes to the live broadcast of a major sporting event. Of course, that doesn't always prevent technical problems from happening. The 2013 Super Bowl in New Orleans, when the lights went out in the Superdome, and Game 1 of the 2015 World Series, when Fox lost its television feed, are just two recent examples of the best laid plans going awry. The network assured us that if we had any kind of power problem that an auxiliary system would kick in and keep us from going off air.

As first pitch neared, Al, Tim, and I filed into the cramped metal box that passed for a broadcast booth at Candlestick Park. The booth was bolted onto the ballpark. The actual press box at Candlestick, which was home to both the Giants and 49ers, could be found in a more football-friendly location down the third-base line.

As we hit the 8:00 hour on the East Coast, Al, Tim, and I took our positions in the booth, leaning against the bench we would sit on during the game so that we were facing away from the field. In a real stroke of genius, ABC enlisted venerable actor James Earl Jones to kick off the broadcast with a voice-over of an ode to the game of baseball written by former commissioner Bart Giamatti, who had passed away just a few weeks earlier. Giamatti's words scrolled on the screen, and Jones' rich, deep voice brought them to life. Earlier that year Jones had turned in an iconic performance as reclusive novelist/baseball fan Terrance Mann in *Field of Dreams*, so it really was a perfect intro to the game.

Per our usual routine, Al welcomed everyone at home to the broadcast, an introduction that included an aerial shot of the Bay Area, which Al called "one of the most spectacular vistas on this continent, any continent." Earlier in his career, Al had worked for a few seasons as a play-by-play man for the Giants, so he knew the area well. So did Joe, who was raised in Oakland. After chatting with Tim about what the Giants needed to do to climb back into the series, Al was a few seconds away from throwing it over to me for some comments.

Then I felt a small vibration. I looked over at Al and Tim. They looked alarmed. Al started to turn white. Tim, who already had a pallor to his skin due to illness, appeared almost translucent. As we lost our video feed, viewers could hear Al say, "I'll tell you what, we're having an earth..." He didn't quite get the word "quake" out.

The quake lasted an incredibly eerie 17 seconds. The desk we were leaning on started to tremble. I watched as the light stanchions in the stadium swayed back and forth like a stalk of wheat in the wind, giving off a terrible metallic groan. It felt like a locomotive had passed through the booth. A massive vibration swept over the stadium. I gazed over at Tim, who looked like a guy trying to keep his balance on a surfboard. Joni was sitting in a chair a few feet away with tears streaming down her face. Tim's wife and a few others huddled in the doorway that led to the booth. And there were Joe and Willie standing on the Candlestick mound, presumably thinking that was the safest place to be on a baseball field during an earthquake. Both teams had also streamed out onto the field. Though I had spent grades five through eight in Southern California and knew about the potential for catastrophic earthquakes, I had never actually experienced one. It didn't occur to me as the quake was happening that lives might be in danger.

We had no way of knowing in that moment that the Loma Prieta quake, which measured 6.9 on the Richter scale, would cause so much destruction and death. So when Al continued his audio-only narration of what had just happened, he didn't strike a somber tone. He spoke as someone who, like everyone else in the area, was in shock over just having felt the earth shake.

"I don't know if we're on the air or not and I'm not sure I care at the moment," he said. "Well, folks, that's the greatest open in the history of television, bar none. We're still here. As far as we can tell, we're on the air. I guess you are hearing us, even though we have no picture and no return audio. We will be back, we hope, from San Francisco in just a moment."

We all hoped that the wild ride was over and that only a few dishes had been shattered in the process. But then ABC sent word from New York that we should take precautions and leave the stadium immediately. So that's what we did. But as we exited

JIM PALMER: NINE INNINGS TO SUCCESS

Candlestick and prepared to broadcast from outside the park, fans were streaming in like nothing had happened. They fully expected to watch a baseball game that night. Some eternally hopeful fans out in the outfield stands, hoping to witness the first ever World Series game in San Francisco, had hastily made a huge handwritten sign that read, "If you think that was something, wait until the Giants come to bat." That wouldn't happen for another 10 days.

The earthquake caused dozens of fatalities, thousands of injuries, and somewhere in the neighborhood of $6 billion in property damage. Many of the deaths occurred when the upper portion of a segment of Interstate 880 collapsed, crushing motorists on the lower level. A portion of the majestic Bay Bridge also fell off.

On the night of the disaster, Al provided live reports from outside the stadium until past 11:00 PM local time. When it became clear that the series wouldn't continue for a while, if at all, I left the Bay Area to do some charity work. A writer from *Newsday* accused Al of being insensitive for his "greatest open in the history of television" remark, but that was unfair. We didn't have a Richter scale in the booth, and Al was just reacting to the moment. He made up for his initial flub, if that's what you want to call it, by helming ABC's news coverage of the event for the next week. After his tiff with Dennis about missing the opportunity to promote the football game, Al joked that he would stick it to Dennis by accruing the largest limo bill in ABC history. I think he accomplished that goal, along the way earning himself an Emmy nomination in the news category for his work covering the aftermath of the quake. Like Jim McKay had done 27 years earlier, Al shined in his role as a newsman.

When the World Series resumed on October 27, the A's finished off a sweep of the Giants, an outcome that is just a footnote to a much larger historical event.

8TH INNING

Appreciation

I'M A FAN OF THE MOVIES OF BARRY LEVINSON, A FILM-maker who set many of his films, including *Diner, Tin Men,* and *Avalon* in his native Baltimore. The city served as more than just a backdrop to the action unfolding on the screen. It was a vital character in its own right. I highly recommend checking out these films if you haven't already. They are classics that really capture the rugged working-class spirit of Baltimore and bring to life the type of colorful characters who inhabit the city. Levinson, a huge baseball fan who later in his career invested a share of his movie earnings into an ownership share of the Orioles, also directed *The Natural*, one of the best baseball movies of all time; *Good Morning, Vietnam*, which provided an early comedic showcase for the late Robin Williams; and *Rain Man*, a film that earned Dustin Hoffman an Oscar for his portrayal of an autistic man.

Diner, which came out in 1982, especially resonated with me. *Vanity Fair* magazine not long ago talked about how the movie influenced so much that came after it, everything from *Seinfeld* to *Pulp Fiction*. It's perfectly cast with Steve Guttenberg, Kevin Bacon, Daniel Stern, Tim Daly, and Mickey Rourke portraying a group of friends in late-1950s Baltimore clinging to their youth while standing on the brink of the responsibilities of adulthood. Rourke's character, Robert "Boogie" Sheftell, was based on a real-life Baltimorean I got to know named Leonard "Boogie" Weinglass, a high school classmate of Levinson's who went on to found the Merry-Go-Round clothing retailer, a fixture of 1980s shopping malls.

The scene in the movie that really stands out in my memory involves Guttenberg's character, Eddie Simmons, a rabid Baltimore Colts fan who makes his fiancée pass a Colts trivia quiz before agreeing to walk down the aisle with her. That scene was apparently based on a real-life situation involving Levinson's cousin. *Diner* and the other Levinson movies transport me back to a time and place that remain very special to me. They also remind me and help me appreciate all the interesting people I met over the years in Baltimore.

During my second winter in Baltimore, I got to know a guy named Johnny Wilbanks, one of the most colorful characters I've ever known, and that's saying something, considering all of the oversized personalities I came across during my playing and broadcasting careers. At the age of 21, Johnny lost both his legs while working as a brakeman for the Ohio and Baltimore Railroad. A lot of guys in Johnny's position would have slipped into crippling depression and allowed the workplace accident to define the rest of their lives. But not Johnny. He got fitted with prosthetic legs and used the workers' compensation money he received from the railroad to open Johnny's New and Used Cars.

My first encounter with Johnny came when I was in the market for a used car. A teammate of mine named John Orsino had bought a burgundy 1963 Chrysler 300 from him. It was a good-looking car. One afternoon I walked into Johnny's office in the 4800 block of Hartford Road, not a particularly upscale part of town, and before I could utter a greeting, he shoved a business card in my hand. It read, "Johnny's Used and New Cars. The Walking Man's Friend." He asked me what I was in the market for (something small and cheap), surveyed the inventory on his lot (nothing fit the bill), and then started working the phones (he seemingly knew every car salesman in the tri-state area.) Later that day we were on the road to Mannheim, Pennsylvania, home to the largest wholesale car auction in the northeastern United States. One of his buddies there set me up with a little red Volkswagen that cost $1,350. I kept the car for a year, using it to drive to speaking engagements in the region. On a couple of particularly windy days, I struggled to keep the car in one lane crossing the Chesapeake Bay Bridge. But I got to all the banquets on time and in one piece. Thirteen months after making the purchase, I sold it back to Johnny for $1,325.

Johnny used to wear the same gray suit, white shirt, and black tie every day. Only the type of hat he wore changed from season to season from a Stetson in the winter to a straw Panama in the warmer months. He always walked around with a huge wad of cash in his wallet and had enough money socked away to make a serious bid at one point to purchase the Orioles. Johnny's first passion was cars. His second passion was baseball. He sponsored a collegiate summer baseball team (appropriately called Johnny's) that brought some of the nation's best amateur talent to the state. Reggie Jackson and Al Kaline were two of the future major leaguers who suited up for Johnny's, a team managed by longtime Orioles scout Walter Youse.

Johnny liked to hobnob with professional athletes, who came from all over the country to do business with him, but he never lost his touch for the common man. He sold a lot of cars to African Americans, which wasn't a very popular thing to do in the 1960s. After making the sale, he'd invite the buyer over to a local bar called Nate and Leon's for a sandwich and a beer. As *The Baltimore Sun* noted in Johnny's 1999 obituary, he offered warranties on his cars and was reluctant to repossess, always trying to work out a reasonable payment plan before taking a car back.

This was the Baltimore I grew to love and still do. And it's because of people like Johnny Wilbanks that I never played anywhere else. Baltimore became a part of the fabric of my life. I got to know all the neighborhoods. The predominately Jewish suburb of Pikesville and the ethnic enclaves of Germantown and Little Italy exuded an incredible sense of community. By virtue of the number of years I spent in town, I came of age with a lot of Baltimoreans.

Baltimore had great people like Pam Pitts, who tutored at the school my daughters attended. My daughter, Jamie, struggled academically until Pam took the time to work with her and understand her learning style. Jamie has always had tremendous auditory skills. When she hears information, she grasps it a lot more quickly than when she reads it. Pam tutored both my kids and put them on the path to academic success. And my kids weren't the only ones whose lives were changed by Pam.

I once ran into a former classmate of my daughters at a Baltimore barbershop. As a teenager he really struggled in school. I hadn't seen him in years, so I guess I just assumed that he didn't take an academic path in life. Boy, was I wrong! He told me that he had just graduated second in his law school class and he credited his success to Pam Pitts. "She taught me how to learn," he said.

In 1984 I went out to dinner in Little Italy with Pam. We decided to try a new place called Da Mimmo's that had opened a few months earlier. We poked our heads in the door to see what the place looked like. All the empty tables that night suggested the restaurant might not survive much longer. We started off back down the street, but Mary Ann Brulinski, a veritable one-woman show who welcomed diners when they walked through the door and waited and bussed tables, chased us down. "Jim Palmer!" she exclaimed like we were old friends. "I used to be a Junior Oriole and wait for you to sign autographs after games. But you never got to me. You can make it up to me by eating at my restaurant." I admired Mary Ann's hustle, so we went back in. After enjoying a delicious meal cooked by chef Mimmo Cricchio himself, we continued talking with Mary Ann, who was still an avid Orioles fan. Little did we know that they were down to their last $800 and had sold one of their cars just to keep things going another couple of weeks. And they would have sold both cars if Mimmo didn't need it to drive down to the market to purchase produce every morning. Barring a miracle Da Mimmo's was going out of business, and the first floor of the row house that it occupied would revert back to a living room.

A funny thing happened the next day. Laura Charles, the long-time gossip columnist for *The Sun* called to see if I had any leads for her "For Your Eyes Only" column. "Hi, Cakes, anything going on?" she asked.

"Well, I just had the best meal of my life last night in Little Italy. The place is called Da Mimmo's."

Laura put the endorsement in her column, and the restaurant's fortunes soon changed. Locals flocked to Da Mimmo's to check it out for themselves. In 1986 Mary Ann and Mimmo got married at the Hands Across America charity event. They also bought a couple of neighboring row houses and expanded the restaurant, which remains a thriving establishment.

Here's the thing about that story. I didn't do Mary Ann and Mimmo any special favor by endorsing their restaurant. I simply told the truth. It was an incredible meal. And people needed to know about the place. And my celebrity allowed me to spread the word.

I'll never understand people whose default setting is rudeness. Why would someone act in a boorish manner when the alternative takes no additional time or energy? The best thing about being in the public eye is that there isn't a day in your life when you can't use your celebrity to make a difference. Whether I'm flying around the country or working out in my local gym, people recognize who I am...or who I used to be, at least.

It's a sad statement on where we are as a country, but 21st century America seems to value fame over talent. Never have there been so many people who are famous for simply being famous. I'm not being haughty when I say that. After all, my fame stemmed from the act of throwing a ball with speed and accuracy. I always tried to remind myself of my good fortune, however. Because of the attention given to my baseball career, I had a natural platform to give back. For me that involved acting as a spokesman for charities. I think we all owe it to ourselves to take a step back and appreciate what we have. I understand that life gets busy and stressful. We get racked by worry and experience sleepless nights over personal and professional struggles. I've tried to avoid clichés and oversimplifications in this book, but this point is too important to state any other way: I think we'd be happier as individuals and a society if we engaged in more simple acts of kindness in our communities and workplaces.

As a resident of the real world, I realize that not everybody is receptive to friendliness and generosity. I'll use the following story as an example. I don't begrudge celebrities who have a blanket policy of not giving autographs, but it's something I've never minded doing...with the exception of the rare times I've been physically incapable of lifting my right arm. In 1974 I had my arm in a sling with instructions from the doctor to refrain from engaging in any physical activity, no matter how light. On my way into the stadium one Sunday afternoon, a guy approached me, asking for an autograph. After I gestured to the sling, I saw a profound look of hurt spread across the guy's face. Doctor's orders be damned, I guess I felt like it would be the right thing to accommodate the guy's request. "Okay, I'll sign one," I told the guy, "but I'm really not supposed to use my hand."

His "thanks" had a little bit too much sarcasm on it for my liking, but I had already committed to the autograph. "Hand me your pen," I told him.

"I don't have a pen," he said.

"See ya later, then," I said and started to walk away.

The guy proceeded to berate me, telling me I didn't care about my fans and their feelings. That stopped me in my tracks. "I consider myself a talented guy, but the one talent I don't have is signing an autograph without a pen," I said. "Don't lecture me about not caring about my fans, but thanks for supporting the Orioles."

That story shows that we can't all act with warmth and benevolence all the time, but it was more the exception than the norm. At my core I always felt tremendous gratitude toward the various communities that I was a part of during my time in Baltimore, both inside and outside the walls of the stadium.

I'm glad I played in an era when players developed relationships with the fans who came out to cheer us on. The major league parks of those days had the intimacy of the spring training and minor league parks of today. We got to know the season-ticket holders by name and watched as their young children became teenagers and then adults over the course of many seasons. Long before the memorabilia craze started, we would hand out batting gloves, broken bats, and other equipment to the people who made us a part of their daily lives and in turn became a part of our daily lives. Just to the left of the dugout at Memorial Stadium sat Stanley Levinson, the "Digger," who was of no relation to Barry, ran the only Jewish funeral home in Baltimore. Watching his home team play 81 games a season helped take his mind off of his morbid vocation, I suppose. Way up in Section 34 of the upper deck was Wild Bill Hagy, a cab driver and ice cream truck driver who led the entire stadium in cheers by spelling out "Orioles" with his body. Hagy initiated a boycott of Orioles games in 1985 after the team banned fans from bringing outside beer into the stadium, but he returned in 1995 when Cal Ripken Jr. broke Lou Gehrig's consecutive games streak. He also performed his routine at Cal's Hall of Fame induction ceremony.

Memorial Stadium wasn't a modern venue. Built in 1922 and redone in the 1950s, it didn't have luxury boxes or other amenities. But the sense of history was palpable. In the offseason I would go to Colts games and I was fortunate enough to get to know Colts legend Johnny Unitas—No. 19, the most beloved sports figure of his or any era.

I developed a tremendous affection for the city. That's why it broke my heart in the spring of 2015 to see chaos on the streets of Baltimore in the wake of the death of Freddie Gray, a young African American man who died in the back of a police van. Though this is a book about strategies for realizing your potential in the workplace, I think it's relevant to briefly discuss what can happen at work, home, or in society when relationships break down like they did in Baltimore and other places around the country that have experienced riots and protests in recent years. As I've already said several times, a successful organization is built on trust. Employees trust the organization, and the organization returns that trust. In the inner cities of America, there is a severe lack of trust between citizens and authority figures. The people don't trust the system, and the system doesn't trust the people. And that's a recipe for disaster. It makes me realize how fortunate I was to have a father figure and a stable family.

The violence spread very close to Camden Yards, where the Orioles were playing a series against the Chicago White Sox. Due to the rioting, the teams played an afternoon game that was closed to the public. Gary Thorne and I broadcast the game in an empty stadium, jokingly tweeting, "If you build it, they will come. Just not today." *Saturday Night Live* even did a spoof of us doing the game. I guess you have to find laughs where you can because what happened in Baltimore during those weeks in April and May 2015 was anything but comical. It cut to the core of the challenges we face as a nation.

When you're part of a great organization, your co-workers and bosses become like family to you. The Orioles family has lost a lot of cherished members since my retirement, and any time a former teammate, coach, or manager passes away, I mourn his loss and reflect on the special years we spent together. Once an Oriole, always an Oriole, I guess.

Some deaths hit me harder than others. I was in Minnesota in August 2011 doing an Orioles-Twins broadcast on the Mid-Atlantic Sports Network when I found out that my friend of 35 years, Mike Flanagan, had taken his own life. In the third inning, through my earpiece I could hear our terrific producer Dawn D'Agostino crying. I asked her what was wrong. She told me she'd tell me after the game. I let her know then I didn't want to wait six innings to find out what was happening. She told me Flanny was dead.

I felt sick to my stomach. Part of me wanted to just sit in a corner and cry. The news was incomprehensible to me, and I just wanted to be alone. Another part of me wanted to express what Flanny had meant to me. And I had a unique opportunity to eulogize Flanny to my larger family, the Orioles' fanbase. I don't think I was particularly eloquent on-air that night, but I didn't care. I just tried to convey my raw emotions. Fighting back tears, I talked about how lucky I was to play with Flanny and how lucky all of us were to be part of such a great organization. I am still devastated by Flanny's death.

An Oriole to the end, Earl Weaver died in the company of the team's fans on a baseball-themed cruise ship in January 2013. I got the news from former teammate Scott McGregor, who regularly traveled the high seas with Earl. Scotty said that Earl remained a fierce competitor to his dying day, trying to find any edge he could to win at shuffleboard or ping pong. On the night of his death, Earl had a drink with Scotty in the ship's bar. Earl said he didn't feel well, and when Scotty got up to go schmooze with the passengers, Earl stayed behind. His last words to Scotty were, "Tell everyone that I love them."

Considering how much Earl liked his alcohol and cigarettes, he probably was fortunate to make it all the way to 82. Still, he was the patriarch of the family, and it hurt to know that I would never again see him at Hall of Fame weekends and Orioles reunion events. I think Boog Powell put it best when contacted for comment on Earl's passing by *The Sun*. Boog quipped, "Wherever Earl is now, I'm sure the umpires are saying, 'Oh no, here he comes.'"

We make ourselves and our organizations better when we take the time to grieve the loss and celebrate the memory of those who helped shape us professionally and contribute to our successes. I want every young Oriole who walks into the clubhouse today to know about Flanny's and Earl's legacies and I want them to feel comfortable reaching out to former Orioles like myself who can share institutional knowledge and help instill pride in wearing the uniform.

Without the mentoring and support I received from the Orioles organization, I wouldn't have achieved fame, wealth, and success. I felt it was only right to give back a fraction of what others had helped me earn.

My association with the Cystic Fibrosis Foundation started when I became spokesman for the Maryland CF Foundation in 1970. I had a friend named Jack Burke who had two children with CF, a disease that causes the lungs and digestive system to become clogged with mucus. Later in the '70s, when I first started posing for photos in my Jockey underwear, the company suggested that we capitalize on the popularity of the ads by coming out with a poster. I was a little uncomfortable with the idea of being on the back of bedroom doors and walls across America, but I agreed to do it with the understanding that a portion of the proceeds would go to CF. The posters became a hit in an era where a lot of young men had glamour shots of Farrah Fawcett on their bedroom walls, and a lot of young women went to bed at night with an image of my semi-clad body in the room. Personally, it made buying Christmas presents

Passion and compassion—they are the cornerstones to a life worth living. Jim writes in this chapter about appreciating and feeling appreciated, which to me equates to passion and compassion. Passion for what you do and what you believe is the highest form of appreciating your life. Compassion for others is how you show appreciation.

In this age of narcissism and self-indulgence, an era in which, as Jim writes, we tend to prize "fame over talent," we have lost all perspective. We equate media attention to success and name recognition to heroism. These are false gods, however. Though it may sound incongruous, the root of compassion is feeling appreciated. If we feel like we are treated well, we will in turn want to treat others well. Nothing creates a greater feeling of being appreciated than compassion—for it is humanly true that we reap what we sow.

Compassion also helps direct our passions. A love for what we do and a defense of our beliefs must always be accompanied by a respect for others. Most telling in this chapter are Jim's words about his autistic stepson, Spencer. There is a passion and compassion there that speaks to appreciating and being appreciated in a most profound way.

**—GARY THORNE,
ORIOLES BROADCASTER**

easy: one of my posters and a set of darts.

Sales of the posters generated a lot of attention for the company and for me personally. The whole thing was kind of insane really. And it got me thinking about the nature of fame, success, and opportunity. Because of my appearance and ability to throw a baseball, Jockey picked me to wear its underwear. That offer resulted in a wonderful and long-standing relationship between the company and me. I was helping to sell a quality product that I had worn my whole life, and recognizing my appeal to both male baseball fans and their wives, Jockey compensated me well for my efforts. But I decided that the money I earned as an underwear spokesmodel shouldn't go into my pocket. I felt I owed it to society to do something more worthwhile with those paychecks. I knew how fortunate I was to have two healthy daughters, so it seemed like an easy call to donate proceeds from the poster sales to the cause. Back then the life expectancy of a child with cystic fibrosis was about 12 to 14 years. Now, it's close to 40. It's been extremely gratifying to see the advancements in medical treatment that have enabled children with the disease to live longer lives.

Twenty-five years later, I had a similar epiphany about how I and others commemorate accomplishments. Where I had my three Cy Young awards and four Gold Glove awards, others might have a Salesman of the Year award and a ring recognizing 25 years of service with a company. You can't take it with you. I am sustained by the memories of my career and the camaraderie I have with so many of my former teammates and opponents. I realized not long ago that the awards, while nice, were only collecting dust in my house. I'm sure that the sports memorabilia collectors who bought and kept my stash of awards got a thrill out of having a piece of baseball history. It was a win-win.

A while back, while attending an American Airlines ski event in Vail to raise money for Cystic Fibrosis, I donated one of my Gold Gloves for auction. In a classy move, the winning bidder declined to take my award, explaining that he was happy to simply make a donation to the cause. The proceeds of the sales of another of my Gold Gloves went to an autism organization in Palm Beach County, Florida. As I mentioned earlier, my 19-year-old stepson, Spencer, has autism, and with one out of every 68 children (one out of 42 boys) in this country on the autism spectrum, we certainly need to increase research into the disorder.

Spencer was just a toddler when he got diagnosed with autism. My wife, Susan, remembers the day vividly. She took Spencer to the doctor because he seemed in his own world, wouldn't make eye contact, and slept all the time. The doctor told her that Spencer, her first child, had a very severe case of the disorder and would probably never be able to speak. Susan felt alone and depressed. Back then Autism Speaks and other advocacy groups didn't exist. Susan had to scour the shelves of bookstores to find information about autism. She got Spencer into speech, occupational, and physical therapy programs at St. Mary's Medical Center in West Palm Beach. The therapists did wonders for Spencer and for Susan, who met other parents who were experiencing the same challenges. She didn't feel quite so alone anymore.

I met Spencer when he was six. By that time,he had started to talk and attend school. He's a really smart kid who knows everything there is to know about trains. I've never seen him more excited than on the day we took a trip on the Amtrak Acela from Baltimore to New York City. I feel very lucky that I have had Susan and Spencer in my life. He's a great kid. When the Orioles announced they would unveil a statue of me Camden Yards in July 2012, Spencer offered to introduce me. All of our friends thought it was a bad idea. They thought he would freeze up in front of so many people. But on the day of the ceremony, he stepped up to the mic, and in his best broadcaster voice, said, "Come on, let's give it up, for the No. 22, still the greatest, the most amazing...that's what he told me to say... Jimmmmm Palmer!!!"

The crowd went bananas. I wasn't the only one wiping away tears. He did such a tremendous job.

Spencer will continue to attend a special needs school until he is 21. After that we're on our own. Susan and I both realize that the average person with an autistic child faces enormous emotional and financial burdens. Although autism has received a lot of attention in recent years, there still aren't nearly enough resources for autistic children. Susan has searched high and low for a rec center or day camp for autistic kids in our area to no avail. We hope that the next decade or so will bring advances in diagnosis, prevention, and treatment of autism.

I still have my three World Series rings. Those were different because they represented team success. I wouldn't feel comfortable selling or auctioning off items that so many people worked hard to earn.

Having played my entire career up the road from our nation's capital, I absorbed enough about the electoral and legislative process to know that I didn't have the will or temperament to go that route. In 1998 I accepted an invitation to speak at a National Press Club luncheon about my life in baseball. My appearance kicked off a month at the club that included speeches from U.S. surgeon general David Satcher, Nike CEO Phil Knight, and senator George Mitchell. Satcher spoke about the country's latest public health efforts, Knight about Nike's role in the global economy, and Mitchell about the recently agreed upon Irish peace accord. I had far less consequential matters to discuss. During the Q&A at the end of my speech, someone asked me if I had ever considered going into politics because the governorship of Maryland was available. I jokingly answered that I had designs on becoming the mayor of Juno Beach, Florida, a sleepy community about 15 miles from Palm Beach. That would be about all I could handle.

We all like to be recognized for our accomplishments, so my induction into the Hall of Fame in 1990 was a special moment for me and all of the people who helped shape my life and work. There were times during my career when I didn't feel appreciated. That's the trap you can fall into when you feel like you're putting every ounce of your being into your job—only to hear occasional jeers from reporters or fans. Getting enshrined in Cooperstown with the second highest percentage of votes in baseball history (only Bob Feller got more) was an amazing tribute and honor. It's hard to describe the euphoria I felt when then-commissioner Fay Vincent handed me my Hall of Fame plaque on a rainy Cooperstown weekend. Being inducted in the same class as the great Joe Morgan, who took me deep in the 1977 All-Star Game, just added to the thrill. My mom passed away three years before my induction, but my stepdad, Max Palmer, who had such a profound influence on my life, made the trip from Arizona.

Baltimore is responsible for so many of my fondest memories. The city doesn't get nearly enough credit for its virtues. Many people associate it with crime shows like *The Wire* and Barry Levinson's *Homicide: Life on the Streets*, which paint a less than rosy picture of the city. But think about what the Baltimore area has to offer. You're not too far from the mountains and ocean. Hop on a train and you're in New York City in a little over two hours. It can get cold in the winter, but the climate is balmy compared to cities in New England and the Midwest.

I've never questioned my decision to play my entire career with the Orioles. A lot of people think the grass is always greener somewhere else, but I knew that the grass was pretty green in Baltimore. We had one of the best organizations in baseball. Our winning percentage during the 20 years I was there proves that point. Why would I have gone somewhere else just to make an extra $150,000 a year?

VISIT TO THE MOUND

I read a 2015 article in the business magazine *Fast Company* that posed a fascinating question: How different would our lives be if we completely eliminated complaining from our daily routines?

The article made some valid observations about how many of us have turned complaining into a pastime: "Griping comes naturally for us. During an average conversation, we lob complaints at each other about once a minute, according to research. There's a social reason for that. 'Nothing unites people more strongly than a common dislike,' said Trevor Blake, author of *Three Simple Steps*. 'The easiest way to build friendship and communicate is through something negative…But all of that whining comes with a cost. When we complain our brains release stress hormones that harm neural connections in areas used for problem solving and other cognitive functions."

Just as smoking is banned in most offices, Blake has said that he's banned complaining. "I give them one chance, and if I catch them a second time, that's it for them," he said. Now I'm not sure what consequences await Blake's team members who complain a second time, but the concept is interesting, not to mention one that would have caused me real problems. I never held back from criticizing teammates, my manager, or baseball itself. I spoke out against Reggie Jackson for holding out for a month of the 1976 season, called Boston Red Sox manager Darrell Johnson "an idiot" for leaving me off an All-Star team, and publicly traded barbs with Earl Weaver so many times that I lost count. And I reserved my biggest complaints for my own body, which I felt betrayed me too many times with its various aches and pains.

But think first before you complain to colleagues about how your boss micromanages or your company makes poor decisions. Be conscious of the energy that you will subsequently be creating. Remember that complaining will feed the monster/problem and often will serve no purpose other than to connect you with others in a negative and disempowering way. In some cases it can be therapeutic and even helpful to air your grievances, though too often the immediate relief we feel from venting our frustrations is outweighed by the risks of your complaints getting back to your boss or CEO. Build the type of professional relationships that allow you to approach your superiors directly with concerns. It's true that my teammates and I bonded over our shared bemusement at Earl's antics. I guess that was a form of complaining. But our complaints about Earl remained playful and were far outweighed by our feelings of trust, respect, and appreciation for the man.

If you're the boss, make sure that you create a culture and environment where your employees feel they can come to you with concerns. Have an open-door policy. Embrace the fact that your employees feel they can come to you and make every effort to understand and appreciate their world.

Rather than trying to abstain from complaining for an entire month, as the *Fast Company* piece suggests, I propose we pay more attention to appreciating the people around us and the situations we experience. I think complaining in moderation can be healthy, but if it's not counterbalanced by appreciation, then we're likely to feel dissatisfied.

A 2012 article in *Harvard Business Review* discussed the importance of expressing appreciation in the workplace. "Feeling genuinely appreciated lifts people up," wrote Tony Schwartz, a CEO and author. "At the most basic level, it makes us feel safe, which is what frees us to do our best work. It's also energizing. When our value feels at risk, as it so often does, that worry becomes preoccupying, which drains and diverts our energy from creating value."

When there is mutual appreciation and respect between managers and employees, trusting relationships develop, lines of communication stay open, and problems get solved more quickly. Everyone responds well to the words "good job." Saying it to others makes it more likely that you'll hear it in return.

This is a book about professional growth and development, but I don't think it's possible to completely separate the personal from the professional. It serves to reason that people are more likely to be happy at work if they're satisfied with life as a whole. Some of the strategies that can be used to make you happier at work also apply to the home and personal setting.

It's easy to get bogged down by the personal, financial, and emotional frustrations of life. When that happens, dissatisfaction becomes our default setting, and a negative mind-set sets in that affects every part of our being. As a result, we become less effective spouses, parents, and workers. We hear a lot of talk about the pitfalls of bringing your work home with you, as if the home is a refuge from all the stresses of the world. But what about the dangers of taking your "home" to work with you? That's just as real of an issue. In particularly difficult times, it's important to reflect on what and who you appreciate.

9TH INNING

Enjoyment

I WON A LOT OF GAMES IN MY CAREER. AND SO DID MY team. But as I hope I've conveyed in the preceding "innings," I also had a heck of a lot of fun along the way. That's because I loved what I was doing. Who wouldn't, right? I was a grown man playing a child's game and getting paid to do so. Especially in times of anxiety and struggle, I always tried to remember that.

Some people live to work. Others work to live. Then there's the vast majority of us who fall somewhere in between. If you like what you do for a living, and I hope that's the case, I think it's important to enjoy your workplace experience. There's a link between happiness and productivity, and I credit much of my success to workplace camaraderie and an ability to never take myself too seriously.

Helping sell underwear, home loans, and nutritional supplements is mostly serious business, so it was a great thrill to have the opportunity to appear on the silver and small screens in other more comedic roles. In 1988 I got to play a baseball announcer in *The Naked Gun*, one of the all-time classic comedies. Parodying the trend of one and two-man booths becoming three-man announcing booths, I'm part of a ridiculous seven-person booth, including Curt Gowdy, Jim Palmer, Tim McCarver, Dick Vitale, Mel Allen, Dick Enberg, and Dr. Joyce Brothers. In 2012 I made a cameo in the HBO series *Veep*, appearing alongside then-Orioles pitchers Jake Arrieta and Tommy Hunter in an episode partly shot at Camden Yards. The great Julia Louis-Dreyfus plays the title role in the show. In our scene an aide to Julia's character, vice president Selina Meyer, is introducing us. "That's Jake Arrieta. He's a starting pitcher," the staffer tells her. "And on his left, that's Tommy Hunter. He's a starting pitcher. Oh, and that's Jim Palmer. He's a Hall a Famer. The guy's a legend. He's a starting pitcher as well."

After getting this information, the sometimes dim Meyer reams out her subordinate. "You don't have multiple starting pitchers," she yells. "There's one mound. Do you see three mounds or one mound?"

I like to think I'm able to laugh at myself. I'm not perfect and I have my foibles just like anyone else. I'll be the first to admit that I have a bit of an obsessive-compulsive personality. I think my repetition of the same routines and attention to detail worked to my advantage during my playing career, but I'm sure my tendency to want everything just so probably rubbed some people the wrong way. I'm thinking specifically of fielders whom I moved from one place to another based on my knowledge of a hitter's spray chart.

One of the more humorous manifestations of my mild OCD (some say it's full-blown) is that I'm a total neat freak. In 1991 I made an appearance on *The Oprah Winfrey Show* when she came to film an episode in Baltimore, the city in which she got her big break as a talk show host in the mid-1970s. Oprah's time in Baltimore is worth talking about because it helps explain her evolution from a young broadcast journalist with talent and drive to one of the most recognizable and admired people in the world. Oprah came to town at the age of 22 to help give WJZ, Baltimore's ABC affiliate, a fresh face for its 6:00 PM newscast. The experience was a disaster for her. She never felt comfortable behind the anchor desk partly because she wasn't treated particularly well by the veteran anchorman with whom she was paired. Less than a year after taking the job, the station realized the experiment wasn't working and fired her. A lot of people in her shoes would have packed up their stuff and taken the next bus, train, or plane out of town. But Oprah stayed strong and stayed true to her ambitions. And to its credit, WJZ had the good sense to find a better fit for her within the company. They offered her the co-hosting job on a new talk show called *People Are Talking*. At first she was reluctant to leave the world of news for a more lifestyle-based show, but she excelled at the job. Her work caught the eye of Dennis Swanson, the general manager of the ABC affiliate in Chicago, who went on to become my boss as the president of ABC Sports. He invited her to host a morning talk show in the Windy City. Two years later she was hosting a nationally syndicated talk show. And the rest is history.

Despite the rough start she had there, Oprah always maintained a place in her heart for Baltimore, and the locals who knew her before she became an international megastar came out in throngs to see the taping at the Baltimore Convention Center. The show's producers obviously did their homework because Oprah wasted no time in confronting me about my passion for cleaning. Fortunately, I was ready for it. I compared myself to the Robert Duvall character in the classic Vietnam movie *Apocalypse Now*. In that film Duvall, as Lieutenant Colonel Kilgore, struts across a beach at sunrise and taking a deep whiff of the air, famously states, "I love the smell of napalm in the morning."

"Oprah," I said, "that's exactly how I feel about the smell of Lemon Pledge."

I made Oprah laugh, and she rolled off the couch, which I have to say ranks up there with any of my other achievements.

I hope my friend and former teammate Davey Leonhard watched the show because he could relate. The first time I rode in Davey's car in the mid-1960s, I searched the vehicle high and low for a bottle of Windex to clean off the windshield. I couldn't believe it when he told me he didn't keep any in the car. I assumed everyone did.

Another time I went over to fellow Orioles pitcher Scott McGregor's new house for a team barbecue. I enjoyed spending the afternoon hanging out with my teammates and their families, but I was distracted the whole time by the unevenness of Scotty's lawn. I couldn't help but tell Scotty about my concerns. For the imposition of having to listen to me complain about his grass, I felt it was only right that I do something to fix the problem. So the next morning, I got some heavy equipment, returned to his house, and reseeded his lawn.

Scotty, who has coached at many different levels of the Orioles minor league system, is constantly asked by young players for advice on how to become a big leaguer. In addition to telling them the obvious about working at every aspect of their game, he also emphasizes the importance of humor. "I tell them that you have to develop an incredibly weird sense of humor," Scotty says. "The game can get pretty intense, and some of the criticism can get pretty harsh, and cutting up is the best release there is."

Scotty and I pitched to one of the great humorists the game has ever produced: Rick Dempsey. In addition to being an outstanding catcher, Demper also brought a ton of personality to the team. His parents had made a living in show business; his father was in vaudeville and on Broadway, and his mother was a model for Coppertone, and he must have inherited the theater gene because he knew how to put on a show during rain delays. I'm referring to his "Baseball Soliloquy in Pantomime," in which he'd go out onto the tarpaulin with pillows stuffed under his jersey and his cap askew and perform his rendition of Babe Ruth's called-shot home run, a performance that included a lot of slipping and sliding around on the tarp.

Back when Demper and relief pitcher Sparky Lyle shagged flies during batting practice as members of the New York Yankees, Sparky, who made 899 career appearances without starting a single game, would toss baseballs to fans up in the stands, a practice that back then resulted in a player getting fined. I guess when you spend as much time in the bullpen as Sparky did you have time to daydream because Sparky told Demper that he wanted to entertain fans during a rain delay by going out on the field with a bucket of balls and throwing them to the wet fans. He added that, depending on his mood, he might even consider doing an impersonation of Babe's famous 1932 home run against the Chicago Cubs.

Sparky never followed through on his vow, but Demper liked the idea enough to try it out himself and make it his own. He debuted his act in Boston during our final game of the 1977 season, which was against the Red Sox. Both teams and their fanbases needed a laugh. Sometimes great seasons go unrewarded. Entering play that day, Boston had 97 wins, and we had 96, but neither of us had a shot at catching the Yankees to win the division crown. During warm-ups Rick had befriended some Red Sox fans, who, despite having to endure coming up short to the Yankees again, still managed to maintain a festive mood.

When it started pouring during the game and the umps called on the ground crew to bring out the tarp, many of the Red Sox faithful started heading toward the exits. Demper decided to give them a reason to stay. Maybe if he had been in the starting lineup that day, he would have thought twice about trying out his act. But Earl had given him the day off, so the stars had aligned.

To a raucous ovation, Demper started sliding on the tarp. Not missing a beat, the Fenway organist provided him with musical accompaniment, banging out "Raindrops Keep Falling On My Head." Demper led the stadium in a sing-along. Soaking wet and clearly having the time of his life, he concluded his show with a wave and a bow before going to dry off. The whole thing was so unexpected that I don't think Earl knew how to react. And he didn't have time to express an opinion anyway because right after Demper returned to the clubhouse, the fans started banging on their seats and chanting, "We want Dempsey! We want Dempsey!" Rich Dauer, our second baseman, came from the dugout to report that the fans demanded an encore and were on the verge of knocking rickety old Fenway to the ground if they didn't get one. Like a rock star, Demper reemerged from the tunnels and continued his show with a Babe impression. Then, much to the joy of the Red Sox fans, he did a dramatic interpretation of Carlton Fisk's home run against the Cincinnati Reds in Game 6 of the 1975 World Series.

Demper expanded his act somewhere along the way to include a parody of yours truly and my role as a Jockey model. The heartiest laughs came when he got our teammate Sammy Stewart to come out onto the field with his underwear on the outside of his uniform.

On the day in May 1978 when I won my 200th game, Demper was behind the plate, calling his customary great game but struggling to break out of a hellacious hitting slump. I believe he had one hit in his last 43 at-bats, and in his third time up that night in the eighth inning, he hit a scorching line drive to right-center that looked like a sure double until right fielder Jim Norris speared the ball in the gap.

Demper could hardly contain his frustration when he came out to catch the bottom half of the inning. When my first pitch to the leadoff hitter nipped the corner of the plate but was called a ball, Demper turned around and told umpire Durwood Merrill that the pitch looked pretty good. Merrill didn't appreciate the critique. "Say one more word to me and you're out of this game," he informed Demper.

"Durwood, the way I'm going at the plate these days, you'd be doing me a huge favor by tossing me from the game."

The Oriole teams I played on in the late 1970s and early 1980s had a lot of talent and heart. That's the main reason we won so many ballgames. But we also had amazing camaraderie. We worked together, played together, fought together, and, most of all, laughed together.

Earl Weaver was our favorite target. He was a guy who loved to go on the offensive and dish it out, so it entertained us to no end to put him on the defensive. He was always the last guy to get on the team bus after road games. It became a running joke for guys on the team to do an Earl impersonation as he boarded the bus. John Lowenstein and Pat Kelly were the best at it. We also liked to mimic his gravelly cackle. Earl would get so mad when we did that.

The Orioles at that time were a perfect blend of veterans and young talent. We were a rare group of guys who got along well and knew exactly when to bear down and win games and when to have fun. That is the recipe for a championship team.

Given the pressure of playing for Earl every day, we all needed those times together to let off a little steam. Because we won so many games, we had the freedom to have more fun than the average team. Although I wasn't the only prankster on the team, I probably spent more time thinking of the crazy things I could get away with than the other guys… only if we were winning, of course. We had a lot of good clean fun. We booby-trapped hotel rooms, "stole" each other's cars, and entertained each other with impressions. When all was said and done, we were left with a lifetime of memories—both of winning games and having a great time.

—RICK DEMPSEY, 24-YEAR MAJOR LEAGUE VETERAN
AND 1983 WORLD SERIES MVP

The joke didn't land with Merrill, who ejected Demper from the game. I couldn't believe it. Here I was on the verge of a milestone victory, pitching a shutout, and I had lost my catcher. Fortunately, we went on to win the game 3–0, so Demper and I can and still do laugh about that night.

Even the teammates who took themselves very seriously indirectly produced some laughs. On his first road trip with us in 1976, Reggie Jackson boarded a Milwaukee-bound flight in a nice pair of designer jeans, Gucci loafers, a grey Gucci sweater, and a Raphael leather jacket. No one could dispute that he looked sharp. No one but Earl, that is. As Reggie walked past Earl's seat in the front row of first class, Earl stood up and curtly reminded him that the Orioles had a strict coat-and-tie rule on road trips, a vestige from the days when the team was managed by Hank Bauer, who had to follow a similar rule when he played for the Yankees. Rules were meant to be broken, or at least bent, so Reggie probably could have gotten away with wearing a sports coat sans tie, but the flashy leather jacket was too much for Earl to overlook. "Wait a minute, Reggie," Earl said, standing up to block Reggie's way, as if that was a real impediment to Reggie advancing into the coach cabin. "You can't go with us to Chicago unless you have a tie on."

"I don't own a tie," Reggie replied, thinking he had outsmarted the little genius.

"You do now," Earl fired back, reaching into the airplane closet and producing a tie. "If you want to go with us, put it on."

Reggie didn't back down, much to the delight of the writers who traveled on the team plane in those years. "That's not how we did it in Oakland," he informed Earl.

And before Earl could utter the words "Well, you're not in Oakland anymore," Reggie proceeded to rattle off the retail price of all of his garments: pants ($125), loafers ($195), shirt ($150). For good measure, he lifted up his sleeve to reveal a $10,000 gold Rolex watch. "Are you saying I don't look good enough to get on this plane?" Reggie asked.

Yes, that's exactly what Earl was saying. Feeling like he made his point, Reggie wrapped the tie around his neck and went to his seat.

The next day, Tony Muser, a journeyman who finished his career with 556 fewer home runs than Reggie, decided to have a little fun at our new teammate's expense. He boarded the team bus with homemade price tags attached to all of his clothes. Shirt: $4. Pants: $6. Shoes: $2.

Almost everybody on the bus got a kick out of Tony's joke, but I don't think Reggie found it all that amusing. That was fine. We didn't bring him to Baltimore for his sense of humor. And I didn't care if he cracked a smile all season as long as he hit a lot of home runs.

Winning is the result of a lot of focus and hard work. But one of the greatest rewards of success is enjoying it. It's easy to relax and have fun when you're winning. Conversely, losing breeds negativity and tension. I saw a lot of Orioles games in 1988 when they dropped their first 21 games of the season, the longest losing streak in American League history. That ended up being a 107-loss season for the club, a number of defeats that it usually took us two seasons to reach in the 1970s. That clubhouse wasn't a fun place to be.

The following season I tried my hand at doing play-by-play for Orioles games. No longer only responsible for making pithy observations between pitches, I was now on the hook for narrating the minutiae of every game. My first game as the voice of the Orioles couldn't have gone worse. Suffering from a nasty head cold, I fumbled my way through the broadcast. Of course, the game against the Red Sox went into extra innings, prolonging my agony. Craig Worthington mercifully ended things in the 11th with a game-winning single. The next day in *The Washington Post*, Tony Kornheiser wrote that the game had produced a proverbial good news/bad news scenario. The good news was that the Orioles weren't in danger of losing their first 21 games again. The bad news, he wrote, was that if I had been pitching and not broadcasting, I would have been relieved in the second inning. It was a great line, and I have to admit it couldn't have been more true.

In his Hall of Fame speech in 1996, Earl acknowledged me twice, first introducing me as, "the gentleman I had more arguments with than my wife," and the second time to make sure he included me on a list of the best pitchers of my era. "I don't want to forget Jim Palmer, or he'll write another bad book about me," Earl quipped.

I admit I was a little hard on Earl in that first book I wrote, but I hope this one more accurately reflects the dynamics of our relationship. As much as we got on each other's nerves, we found a way year after year to work collaboratively. And I attribute that to both of us having a healthy sense of humor. We liked to poke fun at each other, but we also knew how to poke fun at ourselves. I married my wife, Susan, during Hall of Fame weekend in 2007. We had the ceremony at the boathouse of Hall chairwoman Jane Forbes Clark and only invited a few people to attend. When I asked Earl to come, he thought I was kidding.

Ralph Salvon's name isn't all that well-known outside of the Orioles family, but as our head trainer for many years, he and I forged a close relationship. He's the one who discovered I had a torn rotator cuff in 1968. Throughout the 1970s and into the '80s, Ralph and I would drive down to spring training together, leaving Baltimore before dawn to make the 16-hour car trip down to Miami. On the way we'd stop at the original Hardee's fast food restaurant in Rocky Mount, North Carolina, for hamburgers and a game of catch in the parking lot. Ralph and I shared a lot of laughs together over the years.

My best memories of playing in the majors involved sitting on the bench with Scotty, Ralph, and Mike Flanagan, watching the game intently but having a great time, too. Flanny had a wonderful sense of humor and loved to make Scotty crack up. He liked to make up his own versions of the songs that played over the stadium PA system. He'd make corny puns based on players' names. Earl didn't mind hearing us cackle like schoolboys...unless of course we were behind in a game. "What the hell's wrong with you guys?" Earl would yell in such situations. "We're losing!"

"It's this guy," Scotty would say, pointing to Flanny. "He won't stop. He makes me laugh."

After all these years, I can still hear that laughter.

VISIT TO THE MOUND

Don't take yourself so seriously. Easier said than done, right? One of the very reasons people are successful is because they take themselves and what they do seriously. The challenge is not taking the all-business attitude to an extreme and leaving room in one's professional life for humor. Now that can be tricky because not everyone finds the same things funny, and it's easy to cross the line from funny to mean or inappropriate. So I'm not suggesting you go into work tomorrow and put a whoopee cushion on your boss' chair or make fun of the guy in accounting because he has hair plugs. Although I'm not downplaying the importance of sharing occasional laughs with co-workers, I think the real value of humor as it pertains to success in the workplace is the ability to find the silliness and absurdity in our day-to-day routines. As much as you might want to kick the malfunctioning copy machine or scream at the colleague who walks through the hallways whistling, why not take a deep breath and have a good chuckle at whatever's bothering you? Instead of hitting "send" on that argumentative email about the loud talker in your office, take a deep breath and smile at the pettiness of the situation.

It was Robert Frost (sorry, all you Jimmy Buffett fans out there) who said, "If we couldn't laugh, we would all go insane." The ability to laugh at ourselves and our circumstances keeps us on an even keel and less likely to let minor irritations grow and fester.

EPILOGUE

L ONG BEFORE WE SETTLE INTO A CAREER, WE START preparing ourselves for professional success. In baseball you learn your craft in the minors. In life you learn your craft in classrooms. With the proper guidance, encouragement, and mentoring, we can all reach our potential. In the absence of those forces, we run the risk of languishing and asking ourselves later in life what might have been.

Establishing yourself in a field can sometimes be the most difficult part because you can't flash your credentials if you don't have any. With a lot of ability and little luck, you can get your foot in the door...and then bust it wide open. The hard times we face during our careers really do make us stronger. It forces us to dig deep for a resolve we didn't know we had.

Your ability can take you far, but all the talent in the world can't make up for poor interpersonal skills. How well you work with others and how well they work with you is a vital part of workplace success.

True excellence tends to come to those who follow the aforementioned steps. It then becomes a question of achieving at a high level and sustaining that level of achievement over a long period of time. Maybe you have an itch you want to scratch or maybe you'll be forced at some point to dive into a new career. Either way, that can be an intimidating prospect. But thinking about career diversification is important, especially in today's job market. Lastly, take the time to appreciate and smile. You'll be happier at work and you'll be just plain happier.

Who's the winningest Latin American pitcher in baseball history? Juan Marichal? Nope. Pedro Martinez? Guess again. Luis Tiant? Wrong. The answer is my former teammate Dennis Martinez, who, despite never winning more than 16 games in a season, finished with 245 career victories. From 1978 to 1985, a period in which the Orioles appeared in two World Series and won one, Dennis helped anchor the starting rotation. I watched his development in Baltimore with more than a passing interest. His talent was overwhelming. And because he was the first Nicaraguan-born player to reach the majors, he had a great back story. After he had established himself as a capable big league pitcher, he fell into a rut that changed his

> During my senior year of high school, I was wooed by the New York Yankees. Hall of Fame catcher Bill Dickey, an Arkansas native who won eight World Series in Yankee pinstripes, would drive two hours to my family's Memphis home and deliver freshly caught fish to my parents. It gave my mother a delicious Friday night meal to prepare and it gave her son, an aspiring catcher, a chance to pick the brain of one of the all-time greats. I remember Bill telling me to be a friend to my pitchers by supporting them but also by being willing to tell them things they may not want to hear.
>
> Despite those memorable visits to my home, I chose to sign with the St. Louis Cardinals in 1959. And as fate would have it, there I was five years later playing on a team that beat the Yankees in the World Series.
>
> I played the first 10 years of my career with the Cardinals, a franchise that has finished in last place only one time since 1919. The teams I played for in the 1960s had a wonderful stubbornness. Every man on the club aimed for perfection. I had the honor of catching Bob Gibson and Steve Carlton (with the Cardinals and Philadelphia Phillies, respectively), both of whom I consider among my top friends in life.
>
> Like Jim, I transitioned to the broadcast booth after retiring as a player. In Philadelphia I was the fifth broadcaster on a four-man crew, but things changed rapidly when in 1983 I started working for the New York Mets. Then, in 1985 I worked my first World Series, replacing Howard Cosell, starting a decade of memories working with Jim and the indomitable Al Michaels. I thought it might bother Jim to share airtime with another former player, but he welcomed me with open arms to the booth. There is no business quite like the business of baseball, but the lessons of the game are universal.
> —TIM MCCARVER, 21-YEAR MAJOR LEAGUE VETERAN
> AND A MEMBER OF THE BROADCASTER'S WING OF THE HALL OF FAME

approach to the game. He was no longer relaxed on the mound and seemed to treat every game like it was a three-inning audition, showing the first hitters of a game every pitch in his arsenal rather than taking the long-haul approach of saving some of his best stuff for a timely moment later in the contest. Before he left Baltimore for Montreal in 1986, I told him that his overemphasis on trying to dazzle hitters was hampering his ability to be successful.

Dennis figured it out with the Montreal Expos, and I witnessed his evolution firsthand during a *Monday Night Baseball* broadcast in June of 1987. Against the defending champion New York Mets, Dennis pitched a brilliant three-hit shutout. In the clubhouse after the game, we talked about what he had learned about pitching. "I see the whole now," he told me. The whole is made up of many parts, of course, but if you fail to see the big picture, you'll have a difficult time achieving your goals.

When you are in the right workplace environment, it's amazing what can happen. My former teammate, Steve Stone, and his unbelievable 1980 season illustrate that point perfectly. Prior to signing with the Orioles as a free agent after the '78 season, Steve had been a slightly above average pitcher with the San Francisco Giants, Chicago Cubs, and the Chicago White Sox. His best season with the White Sox, a 15-win campaign in '77, looked a lot less favorable when considering it featured a 4.51 ERA. Steve threw a variety of pitches, including a big sweeping curveball and a decent enough fastball that he could locate pretty well. To take his performance to the next level, he just needed to work in the right place. Steve was amazed at how much we cared about winning...and about each other. At his previous stops, his teammates were constantly trying to outdo each other. In Baltimore we maintained a sense of friendly competition, but never did it come at the expense of helping each other. We told Steve to master his curve, fastball, and change-up and eliminate the other pitches from his repertoire.

In his first season in Baltimore, he didn't pitch deep into many games and took a lot of no-decisions. But that one year with Rick

Dempsey as his backstop set him up for one of the greatest breakout seasons in baseball history. At spring training Demper encouraged Steve, who was 32 at the time, to concentrate on getting ahead in the count and then getting hitters to strike out on bad pitches. "Don't worry about throwing the ball in the dirt," Demper told him. "It'll never ever get by me. I promise I'll never miss it." Demper more or less lived up to his promise, helping Steve earn a career high in strikeouts in '80. Steve also benefitted from the tremendous fielders playing behind him.

Here's another trivia question for you: what pitcher won the most games in a season for the Orioles? Answer: Steve Stone. His 25–7 mark in 1980 earned him the American League Cy Young award, making it the fifth time in eight years that an Orioles pitcher won the honor. We'll never know if Steve would have sustained that success for years to come because an elbow injury ended his career the next season.

When a new pitcher joined our club, he knew he had a top-notch defense playing behind them. He worked with catchers, who knew how to call pitches and with coaches and teammates, who knew how to evaluate opposing hitters. That formula helped Steve have his career year, and it explains why I enjoyed as much success as I did.

The workplace can shake your faith and self-confidence because it's almost always a place where you're judged on how you do (or how someone perceives you're doing) and not on what kind of person you are.

If you're out on the mound and meet eyes with a coach who texted you the night before to tell you what a failure you are, you might start to question your own ability and grip the ball a little tighter. If you're in a cubicle and your boss berates you for under-performing, you might have a crisis of confidence. Imagine the alternative. A boss communicates to his team, "Okay, this is what we're going to do today. I really believe in all of you guys. Let's keep trying to get a little bit better."

That was "The Oriole Way."

There's a natural order to our professional lives when things are going well. Hall of Fame third baseman George Brett talks about how the baseball looked like a beach ball the season he hit .390. He didn't feel uptight. He knew what he could do and couldn't do. I observed the same self-assurance in Jake Arrieta of the Cubs in the 2015 postseason. Jake, who spent three undistinguished seasons with the Orioles before getting traded to Chicago, has blossomed into one of the best pitchers in the game—not because he developed new pitches but because he got to a better place mentally. Wouldn't it be nice if we could all experience that kind of serenity in the workplace?

As a pitcher I learned to do my job one batter at a time. That took preparation that included watching film and studying batters from the bench. In other lines of work, you do a job one task at a time. Every game was a blank canvas. Every day is a blank canvas. For the entirety of my baseball career, I tried to paint nine-inning portraits. Then I went off to seek new adventures and challenges. I encourage you to do the same thing.

ACKNOWLEDGMENTS

JIM PALMER

I would like to thank my family for their love and steadfast support. My wife, Susan, and stepson, Spencer, provided me with great inspiration as I worked to put this book together. And to my daughters, Jamie and Kelly, all I can say is that I'm incredibly proud to be your dad.

You don't get into the Hall of Fame alone. It's an organizational accomplishment. And I feel enormous gratitude toward Cal Ripken Sr., Earl Weaver, and George Bamberger for teaching me "The Oriole Way." Peter Angelos and his sons, Louis and John, have embraced that tradition and understand how important baseball is to the people of Baltimore. My appreciation for them is deep. Thanks also to all the people who have worked behind the scenes to help make the Orioles organization so special.

Thanks to my bosses and co-workers at MASN for the opportunity to stay involved with an organization that shaped who I am.

I'm grateful to the people who helped me find a fulfilling life after baseball. Bill Herrmann at Jockey International trusted me to work for him for 19 years. Bob and Troy Henderson and David Moore gave me a similar opportunity at Nutramax.

Thanks to Ric Bachrach for all his support and guidance. This book would not have been possible without Ric's efforts. Thanks also to Roy Firestone and Brad Kaufman for reviewing my manuscript and giving me feedback and to Roy for writing the foreword. My co-author, Alan Maimon, was a pleasure to work with. Thanks to Jeff Fedotin at Triumph for taking the manuscript and bringing us to the finish line. Thanks to Michelle Scarafile for her help in the "Visits to the Mound" sections. Thanks to Richard Marra, Doug Kass, Buck Showalter, Dennis Eckersley, Dr. Bob Henderson, Frank Blethen, Brooks Robinson, Dan Shaughnessy, Ken Singleton, Gary Thorne, Rick Dempsey, and Tim McCarver.

ALAN MAIMON

Thanks to Tom Bast and Mitch Rogatz at Triumph for bringing me in on a book that I hope both entertains and inspires.

Thank you to the Orioles public relations department for providing photos and other assistance on the project.

Chuck Myron, as he's done so many times before, helped me organize my thoughts and made sure I stayed on the right track.

Thanks to Rick Dempsey, Dave Leonhard, and Scott MacGregor for sharing their memories of playing with Jim.

The incredible repository of information at Baseball-Reference.com, the in-depth coverage of the Orioles at *The Baltimore Sun*, and Tom Boswell's columns for *The Washington Post* helped put Jim's career into context.

Thanks to the great people at Centurion Ministries. I am proud to work with you. I am lucky to have such supportive parents, so thanks, Mom and Dad. Thanks, finally, to my wife, Angela, and our daughters, Annabelle and Rosie. Hugs and kisses to you all.